CW01643076

FORTHSPRING 5 DECADES PROJECT

TALKING ABOUT THE TROUBLES

Published in 2014 by Forthspring Inter Community Group

ISBN 978-0-9929478-1-1

First Edition
First Impression

Designed by April Sky Design, Newtownards
www.aprilsky.co.uk

A catalogue record for this book is available from the British Library.

Acknowledgements

5 DECADES is a project supported by the European Union's PEACE III Programme, managed for the Special EU Programmes Body by the Community Relations Council/Pobal Consortium. Thanks to Graham Parkinson and Patricia Armstrong from SEUPB for their support.

The Project Advisory Group: Jenny Meegan, Claire Hackett, Peter Collins, Jessica Blomkvist, Eamonn Baker.

The Storytelling facilitators: Patrica McQullain, Kay Nellis, Philip Cahill, Karen McCartney, Padraig O Tuama, Jenny Young.

The Belfast Telegraph for supplying front covers and a number of images.

Organisations who supported the project including: Towards Understanding and Healing, Healing Through Remembering, Forthspring Inter Community Group, Woodvale Methodist Church, Clonard House, Owenvale Court, Tar Anall, New Life City Church, Cambria Street, Belfast City Council, Falls Library, Shankill Library, Whiterock Library, Central Library Newspaper Library, Alchemy Design, St. Louise's Comprehensive College, Kestrel Print, YouthAction.

The staff and Board of Forthspring for all their support, including Youth Matters and Springers for engaging so readily with the project.

Ruairi O'Connor for transcribing and organising material.

Special thanks to Maura Moore, Director of Forthspring, for all her patience and support for the project.

Finally, and most significantly, heartfelt thanks to each of the participants who shared their own stories and took the time to listen to and seek to understand the stories of others.

And, of course, anyone I have forgotten.

Johnston Price
5 Decades Project
Forthspring

Introduction

In Julian Barnes' novel, 'The Sense of an Ending', precocious schoolboys discuss their understanding of history. For one history is 'the lies of the victors' though he is reminded by his teacher that history also includes 'the self-delusions of the defeated'. The novel moves towards a view of history as 'the memories of the survivors, most of whom are neither victorious or defeated' and ends 'there is accumulation. There is responsibility. And beyond these there is unrest. There is great unrest'.[1]

In the midst of local unrest on Belfast's longest interface, and wider unrest in the body politic, the 5 Decades Project has addressed the task of exploring the legacy of the recent conflict. It has done this through storytelling and dialogue, through the telling and sharing of the memories of some of those who lived through the conflict. The project set out with the objective of acting as a conduit for the narration and hearing of stories. As the stories mounted up into an impressive body of reminiscence it, more and more became clear that each story has its context and is shaped by the life history and the character of the teller. The narrative linking the stories attempts to give some sense of the context by reference to the times the stories emerge from and to the wider social and political backdrop they are set against. It strives, as best it can, to be faithful to the spirit of the individual stories and the storytellers. The project is grounded in the belief that humanity can be found in something as terrible as the conflict that waged so brutally in the North of Ireland from the late 1960s well into the 1990s, and that the humanity is to be found in the detail of individual stories.

Forthspring, based on the Springfield Road, exists as a shared space and has worked since 1997 to build relationships between the neighbouring Protestant and Catholic communities. Part of building relationships is having an understanding of what divides and separates people. In addition to living apart, divided by a peace wall, local people have a very different experience and understanding of the recent conflict. The 5 Decades Project was established with financial support from the EU Peace III programme, administered by SEUPB and the Community Relations Council, to explore the differing experiences and memories of the 'Troubles' with the goal of creating a shared, but not agreed, account of the conflict and its impact

1 Barnes, J The Sense of an Ending

on local people and communities. Shared in the sense that everyone lived through the conflict whatever their particular experience of it and shared also in the sense that people literally sat down with each other and shared their stories, their memories, their hurt and pain and, on occasions, the humour of the conflict.

Initially small groups of people from the same community background came together to share their experiences and memories, moving across the five decades from the 1960s onwards. If people felt comfortable there was the opportunity to share their stories in a larger group, drawn from people of different community backgrounds and/or recording their stories in individual one to one interviews. The emphasis throughout the process was on participants feeling safe. Groups were co-facilitated to ensure careful attention was paid, not only to what was said, but to how participants felt during the sessions, and to ensure that support was always available if required. Within these structures however the approach was informal and relaxed and participants reported that they found the experience not only beneficial but, by and large, enjoyable. Participants valued the opportunity to have their stories told, to hear the stories of others and to recall and work through their memories of what were, often, very difficult experiences. The recordings were, with one exception, carried out on a one to one basis. In each case the interviewer was a facilitator with the project. The majority of the interviews were carried out by the project co-ordinator. The exception was one group who preferred to be interviewed as a whole group. Following the interview the digital recording was transcribed and an edited version of the transcript produced. This edit was given to the interviewees for changes if necessary and the final, agreed version became the material used in the exhibition and this publication. At an early stage it was decided not to use interviewees names. Most participants preferred this and the decision was made on the basis of maximising the number of participants willing to share their stories and to present the stories in a consistent way. The material, as it is presented here, is largely organised in a chronological way, from the '60s to 2000 and beyond, following the five decades the project covered. However, during the group sessions, recurring themes emerged that cut across the whole period of the conflict and the final section considers topics such as the position of women during the conflict, the insatiable appetite for news, the concern for others and the resilience displayed by people.

The project has worked both with existing groups and organizations and with individuals who contacted the project and became part of a group in which they shared their stories. Ages ranged from 16 through to people in their nineties, with the main body of participants aged between 40 and 70. More women took part than men. The groups the project worked with were all based either on the Springfield Road or the wider Falls/Shankill area. To date the project has worked with 146 people drawn from both sides of the peace wall that separates the Falls and Shankill, with a significant representation of both communities in the project.

Older people shared their stories and memories with younger people in a number of events, one extraordinarily well facilitated by members of Forthspring's youth project, Youth Matters, with the support of Youth Action. On a bright spring evening people shared memories of the Troubles, talked about the role of women during the Troubles and, at the end of the evening, released their hopes for the future on balloons that sailed off on a stiff breeze, heading it seemed appropriately towards Stormont and the Castlereagh Hills. An exhibition of the stories was hosted by Belfast City Hall in January and February 2014 and then came back to Forthspring where local school children came, viewed the exhibit, and engaged in discussion with participants in the project who shared their memories.

A central feature of the project has been its location, straddling the interface, always working back and forth with the benefit of operating from the shared space of Forthspring. The name itself drawn from a combination of the Springfield Road and the Forth River. Forthspring, along with the Falls/Shankill area sits beneath the Belfast Hills – Divis and Black Mountain. It was the hills that gave rise to the housing, with the ready water supply flowing off the hills powering the mills that employed the men and women of Shankill/Falls, and gave rise to engineering firms, most notably James Mackie and Sons. The Springfield Road now divides the Falls and Shankill, when it once connected them. The road has gone through a number of dramatic transformations. Initially it connected Springfield Village to Belfast. As the city industrialized at the end of the 19th century the road developed. Large three storey dwellings were built on the front of the road, housing the managers of the new mills and factories. The new inhabitants tended to be Protestant. Springfield Primary School opened in 1910, to be followed in the 1920's by Springfield Methodist Church. James Mackies and Sons was the largest employer in the area, employing a mainly Protestant workforce. By the 1960's the road was a busy, shop lined arterial route that physically connected the Falls and Shankill. All this was to change by the end of the decade. The traditional textile industries began to close in the face of competition from the far east, Mackie's went into what was to prove a terminal decline and civil unrest resulted in rioting, increased segregation and destruction of property.

By the 1980's the road more closely resembled a war zone than a flourishing arterial route. Today it is divided by Belfast's largest and longest peace wall.

It is important to note that the civil unrest and violence that covers the period 1968 to 1998, and rumbles on to this day, was not new to Belfast, or the Springfield Road. This is not a story of a generation that suddenly and inexplicably sundered apart. Belfast has always been a divided city. Andrew Boyd in the classic publication, Holy War in Belfast, demonstrates this clearly. He begins by boldly stating: 'Religious bigotry in Ulster is not difficult to understand'. The answer 'lies in the history of the province where for centuries Catholics and Protestants have fought an endless war of words and politics and, at times, have recourse to the utmost armed violence'.[2] Boyd reports on a weekend's violence in the city in 1886, during which nine people died, one of them in what became known as the Battle of Springfield: 'At one o'clock on Sunday morning rioting broke out in Cupar Street. Protestatants and Catholics, both factions apparently well armed, kept up a continuous exchange of gunfire until daybreak'.[3]

2 Boyd, A Holy War in Belfast (1987) p.1
3 Ibid p.165

CHAPTER 1
1960s

Backdrop – I loved the '60s – The time before the Troubles - Rhyme and Reason – A different world – The Twelfth - God Save the Queen – Location, location, location – James Young – Naked Sectarianism – Springfield Road – The world had turned upside down – Put Out – On the Wrong Side of the Road – Moved Out - Soldiers – The Soldiers – Snow in Derry.

Backdrop: What ever happened to peace, love and understanding?

The '60s was a decade of freedom and youthfulness. It began with JFK as President in the United States. Young people in the West became, for the first time, mass consumers. Free love was made possible by the pill. The new mood of peace and love was allied to new forms of consciousness, aided by the consumption of drugs. The Woodstock festival became the symbol for this altered state. However, the tarnished nature of the 60's dream was to be symbolized in turn by the violence at the Altamont Festival and the end of the idealism that had characterized much of the period. In the words of Joni Mitchell 'They won't give peace a chance that was just a dream some of us had'.

Martin Luther King led the movement for civil rights. Human beings went into space and walked on the moon. The possibility of change was in the air. By the late '60s the defeat of the United States in Vietnam became a symbol of successful resistance to imperial might. The alliance between workers and students across Europe offered the promise of global revolt. Paris in May 1968 seemed to offer the possibility of a whole new social order.

There is a tendency to see the sixties in Northern Ireland as a period of increasing tension that eventually gave rise to the violence, first in Derry, then in Belfast. The memories of many participants recorded here paint a different picture. It's a picture of the sixties as a time of hope and optimism, a time of change. New housing was symbolic of change. Two women now living on the Shankill described their moves from pre-war housing into new builds, one moving from Ligoniel to Ballysillan, the other making the short journey from Brown Square at the foot of the Shankill to the new Shankill Estate. For both of them it was like 'moving into a palace'. The residents of Brown Square moved as a community into the new estate, moving in small groups as new blocks of housing were completed.

It was a time of economic prosperity, at least for those with connections in the labour market, a set of circumstances that favoured Protestants over Catholics, particularly Protestant men. A Shankill Road woman tells of leaving school at 14 on a Friday and starting work on the following Monday in Murray's Tobacco. She was paid off, however, when she was married. This was standard practice at the time.

Early '60s redevelopment in Belfast brought the move from pre-war, inner city housing to new estates like Turf Lodge, Ballymurphy and Highfield. In a time of reduced tension they were religiously mixed areas. There was a sense of the new, of change, hope and optimism. A sense of freedom reflected in music and fashion, the Beatles and miniskirts. The civil rights movement in the United States was an inspiration to campaigners against inequality and discrimination.

In the economic prosperity of the '60s new relationships began to emerge. People from Protestant and Catholic communities not only worked together, they socialized together after work. One participant tells of staff outings to see James Young, the Belfast actor and comedian, as a conscious decision to counter the increasing cracks and divisions appearing in the workplace as tensions rose.

In Northern Ireland the hope and optimism of the '60s sat alongside underlying tensions. In 1964 riots followed an RUC raid on Sinn Féin's election office in Divis Street to take down a Tricolour on display. 1966 marked the fiftieth anniversary of the Easter Rising. Although both governments, North and South, feared a militant response the anniversary gave momentum to political, rather than physical force, republicanism. The violence came from an unexpected direction, loyalism. A month after the Easter Commemorations in 1966 the UVF issued a statement declaring war against the IRA. John Scullion, a Catholic unconnected to the IRA, was killed a month later, the first death of the modern Troubles.

Politically the decade was shaped by the demand from the Catholic minority in Northern Ireland for an end to discrimination in housing, employment and electoral reform. Unionism was dominated by the reformist Terence O'Neill who met Sean Lemass, the Irish Taoiseach in 1966 and the conservative Ian Paisley who organized protests against the civil rights movement. In Westminster the habit was to leave matters Northern Irish to Stormont with the time spent discussing Northern Ireland in Westminster averaging less than two hours per year.[4] But at the end of the decade that was to change dramatically.

4 Taylor, P Provos The IRA and Sinn Féin p.32

The Civil Rights Association became a mass movement following a small protest in Caledon in 1968. A house, allocated to a young, single protestant woman ahead off many Catholic families on the waiting list was occupied by squatters, including the Nationalist MP Austin Currie, protesting against the unfairness of the allocation. The squatters were evicted by the RUC. The eviction gave rise to the first Civil Rights march. The songs of the Black civil rights movement in the USA, including 'We Shall Overcome', were adopted by the marchers. By October a large march in Derry was attacked by the RUC in Duke Street and Northern Ireland was on the world stage. The Unionist administration was caught between demands for reform and reaction. For some there was too little reform, for others too much. Terence O'Neill, the Unionist leader most associated with reform, resigned in April 1969.

Trouble that accompanied the annual Apprentice Boys Parade in Derry in August 1969 quickly developed into what became known as 'The Battle of the Bogside'. CS gas was used for the first time to control a riot in the UK. After three days of rioting, troops were put on the streets.

In Belfast protests against police actions in Derry led to attacks on a number of police stations, including Springfield Road barracks. The following night major rioting broke out in Belfast as Catholic homes were attacked and burnt. The burning of Bombay Street, just off the Springfield Road, remains

a powerful symbol of the threat experienced by the Catholic community. In two nights of severe rioting 5 Catholics and 2 Protestants were killed. Again the army were called on to the streets. Jim Callaghan, responding to a demand to bring in the troops, remarked 'I can get the army in but it's going to be a devil of a job to get it out again'.[5]

According to journalists Patrick Bishop and Eamonn Mallie, by this stage "both communities were in the grip of a mounting paranoia about the other's intentions. Catholics were convinced that they were about to become victims of a Protestant pogrom; Protestants that they were on the eve of an IRA insurrection"[6]. In the mid '60s the possibility of new relationships seemed real and whilst change was to come, it wasn't to be on the basis of agreement or consensus. By the end of the decade the battle lines were firmly drawn. Barricades were erected to defend local areas and re-inforced by the newly arrived troops. The British commander, Lieutenant-General Sir Ian Freeland commented 'The peace line will be a very, very temporary affair. We will not have a Berlin Wall or anything like that in this city'.

Stories of the '60s

It is tempting to read the ensuing conflict back into the '60s and view it as a time of rising tension in Northern Ireland but for many people it was a time of fun, freedom and the possibility of change. But in the stories that reflect this desire for change we can also hear the persistence of a social conservatism and the influence of religious division and sectarianism.

I loved the '60s

I loved the '60s. I loved the dancing – not Irish dancing but the jive! The dances were mixed. I remember these two boys from the Shankill, we called them 'the Billys' because we weren't sure of their names. After a dance one night they tried to kiss my friend and me. We were so innocent! I was 17 and had never been kissed. My friend stopped them and said we weren't like that, and we didn't see them again after that.

5 Taylor, P Provos The IRA and Sinn Féin p.32
6 Bishop,P., Mallie, E, The Provisional IRA, p103

That was ok, but you would never bring a Protestant home to meet the family – we all knew that much! It was a big deal to inter-marry. It broke up families.

Here are the memories of a man who was a child when the Troubles started. For this 10 year old there was little sign of change, the most notable feature of life in the North was the absence of anything happening.

The time before the Troubles

I grew up in a street named Bearnagh Drive and to this day I still live in the Andersonstown area. Bearnagh Drive is a very long street which runs from Koram Ring to the Glen Road. Situated half way up the street was my primary school which was called 'Holy Child Primary School.' I believe the school was once in the Guinness Book of records for being the largest primary school in Western Europe. I think at that time it had about 1400 pupils. The street itself hasn't changed a lot and the school is still there much the same as it was, except there were a lot of kids in the street in those days and we all played together. Now it is much quieter.

Of course we were all Catholic kids and that was taken for granted. The Protestant community never really existed for us back then in Andersonstown and we never gave it a second thought. We never mixed with Protestant children because there weren't any living near us for miles around. Much later I discovered there were some Protestant families living in the Andersonstown area back then but as the Troubles went on they all moved away. I never really met any Protestants until I went to university.

I was born in November 1959 so I was ten when the present conflict started in 1969. Growing up I remember watching reports of the Vietnam War on the T.V. news every night. I knew Vietnam was too far away to affect me, but exciting things were happening there, and I used to look forward to tea and toast for supper in front of the T.V. news reports. As a young boy who enjoyed playing with toy soldiers I found war very exciting. In those days all the kids in the street had toy guns and some had soldier's uniforms. Later on there would be a lot of real guns in the street but we didn't know that then. Looking back I supposed we were kind of obsessed by war and it was all a bit unhealthy. I think this meant we were not so appreciative of the suffering involved in war when things really kicked off. I think to a lot of kids in those days the early part of the troubles were just an extension of playing at war which they had been doing for years.

I was vaguely conscious that people got hurt and died in a war but I didn't spend too much time thinking about the suffering that it involved. The helicopters and the guns and the battles fascinated me but the downside of that was I lived in Northern Ireland. I knew from the geography I had been taught at school that Northern Ireland was part of Ireland but ruled by Britain and situated on the north western edge of Europe. It was a pretty boring place as far as I could tell. In fact I couldn't think of a more boring place to live in the world. I wondered why God had put me on this particular spot on Earth, when I could have been born in so many other places which were far more exciting.

Sometimes a police car went down our street. That was about as exciting as things got before 1969. The police car looked a bit like the same police cars I saw on American T.V. shows but as kids we didn't think very much about the police, who they were or who they represented. On T.V. the police were always the good guys and I suppose we must have thought the same thing applied here too.

It was 1968 and I remember thinking nothing remotely exciting would ever happen here. We would never have a war like Vietnam. Northern Ireland would never be on the TV news. Little did I know then that in the summer of 1969 everything was about to change very quickly, and our little place would be on the news pretty much every night for the next thirty years or so.

However, for this sixteen year old, the sixties was a time of excitement and change, symbolized in an evening of poetry and songs. The title of the event is explained in this extract from Seamus Heaney's memory of David Hammond: 'In 1968 he had toured Northern Ireland with Michael Longley and myself in a programme of songs and poems entitled Room to Rhyme. The title comes from the first verse of a mummers play demanding, "Room, room, my gallant boys, Give us room to rhyme," and the impulse and extravagance suggested by this invocation remained alive in him to the very end'. [7]

Room to Rhyme

It was just a wonderful evening of poetry and song and stories. And I didn't realise, as I was only sixteen years old, that I was in a room where there was greatness because you had Seamus Heaney, Michael Longley and Davy Hammond singing folk songs. They were all about the themes of life, love and death. And as a teenager, my goodness, these are more important than anything else that was

7 Seamus Heaney, Obituary of David Hammond, Guardian 28th August 2008

going on. This must have been, perhaps, '68 – it was before the Troubles, that last autumn before the Troubles. Just listening to the poetry and the lyrics, Michael Longley was so Protestant in his outlook and Seamus Heaney came from a more Catholic/Nationalist/rural perspective. And then the folk songs, well, it just appealed to me in my youthfulness – you know there were all these commonalities and all these universal things that affected us all, and they were bigger than politics, as far as I was concerned. The event took place in Orangefield Secondary school – a boy's state secondary school – would something like that happen now?

Think about the ramifications of all of that because it was 1968; people knew there were things bubbling up. We had a club in school which a lot of schools had signed up to and it was called the Council in World Citizenship. We would invite different people to come and talk to us and somebody in class, a girl from the Shankill, she wanted Bernadette Devlin to come and talk to us, maybe because she knew she was stirring a bit, but I didn't really understand that this was quite a controversial thing to be asking for. I remember being told that we couldn't really do that because it wouldn't go down to well with everybody.

The door was open and the house was dark
Wherefore I called his name, although I knew
The answer this time would be silence
'The door was open and the house was dark'
in memory of David Hammond by Seamus Heaney

For this young woman the '60s were a time of excitement, prosperity and opportunity that retained a sense of innocence.

A different world

It was a completely different world and I honestly don't think that world will come back because it was after the war; there were jobs, there was prosperity – everywhere. I mean you could have left a job on Friday and went into another one on Monday, but for the first time teenagers had money and they were able to do these fantastic things. It was a whole new era from the previous one and there was just so much freedom and so many new things – London was accessible, fashion was accessible and there were places to meet. The other thing that I remember about the sixties was that there were so many dances and places you went where drink wasn't involved. People say you hadn't much to do, but you had this great big opportunity, whereas today, all young people's social places involve drink. So I think in that era, you had a certain amount of innocence. I mean I know some fellows went out to the pub before they went to the dance but they didn't drink in the dance.

Others had, and retain, an attachment to tradition. This woman has fond memories of the Twelfth as a central part of her childhood and her world view.

The Twelfth

My memories start with the 11th night. All the footpaths were painted. The wood was stored in yards until the 11th morning, some was already gathered at the end of the street and then everybody opened their back doors and the wood was taken out. Sometimes they stayed out all night. My mum had got the plastic out of Mackies to put over the hut that they built to keep them dry. And then my Ma was going to beat the brains out of my Da as she had left him the stuff for over the holidays and he had done a fry for all the fellas who had sat out.

On the 11th night we all sat on the footpath. We all had our tatty crisps and our juice. There was a counter taken out of one of the shops and put across the top of the street so no cars could get in. All the women were sat at their doors. Maybe someone brought out an accordion and somebody a flute and they would have played the music. All the kids had to go in and get their ma's pot lids and the old woman at the top of the street did the Indians and all the kids marched round the bonfire. Every street had its bonfire. Old carpet was put up on windows to make sure the windows were not broke. At the end of the night the entry was swept. The women swept the whole entry, they were out with torches. You went in and got washed. Your clothes all left out for the twelfth morning. You got up the Twelfth morning, got your breakfast and your Ma would have made up a lot of sandwiches, filled the flasks. You took your portable seat and went away up the Lisburn Road by the Windsor church. They used to let out seats. You spent your day there. The bands went past. You went to a chippie waiting for the bands to come back. I used to sit and watch, waiting for my Da to come down with his collarette, because I knew once he came down he would take me by the hand to walk part of the road with him. I always remember that. You daren't have broken those ranks, now you see the kids running through, you weren't allowed. They would have broken your legs quicker than let you break the ranks. You came home. My Da would have had a bottle of wee Willie. Neighbours would have sat at the door talking. That was your Twelfth.

When I see the kids with their collarettes it tears the heart out of me yet, for that is the next generation coming up.

But the sixties were also a time of tension and division. This story recalls this in a humorous way. The riots around the removal of a tricolour in 1963 and the sectarian killings around the time of the 50th commemoration of the Easter Rising were more violent and public demonstrations of the underlying tensions and sectarian divisions that lay within Northern Ireland.

God Save the Queen

My husband and I moved into an all Protestant Street in the 1960s. The day we moved in, our neighbours put a radio in the window and played God Save the Queen. We didn't own a radio so I walked down to a shop and explained the story so I could borrow one. The next day I played the Soldier Song out our window. She never bothered us again and we got on real well after that.

Where you lived as well as the outlook of your extended family shaped how you would see the world. This woman points to the contrast between her experience and that of her future husband's, though they both grew up relatively close to each other in the Shankill.

Location, location, location

My husband grew up on the opposite side of the Shankill, up Agnes street, and he would have spent his days after school near his grannies as his parents worked up that way also; so that's what he would have thought as his playground as such when he was growing up. We lived on the other side in Sugarfield Street and if you walk down Sugarfield Street and across Cupar Street it took you straight into the Kashmir Road – and that was our playground. There was also a place where children, both Catholic and Protestant children would have all assembled. We called it the meadow but it was the old run-off of the mills, god knows what was in it. The waste from the mill ran out into it. It was really just a dirty old river with bricks and bits of fish heads lying in it and there were two sorts of slopes or mucky banks ran down to it – and of course that's where we spent all of our time – wet days or dry days, it didn't matter. The "meadow". It was far removed from a meadow. You know in your mind's eye you say the word meadow and it describes a beautiful place. It wasn't a beautiful place but we loved it. We absolutely loved it. So, the Catholic children from the area would have been there with the Protestant children, so we'd have all been playing there anyway. But I remember going up the Kashmir Road to call for people, you know, rap their doors and I also remember swinging on the Clonard gates waiting on people coming out of mass as you'd have called for them while they were at mass and we'd just come down and play outside the chapel waiting on them coming out.

Whereas my husband, growing up a short distance away, he didn't know any Catholics; it was just the lay of the land sort of thing. Just five minutes' walk from our house but that was enough. Agnes Street runs from the Shankill up to the Crumlin Road, you know. It must have been a densely Protestant area, because my husband said he didn't meet a Catholic person until he went to work. And he wouldn't have been brought up in a Loyalist type of household, even though his daddy was a country man and quite often people from the country were quite staunch in their beliefs, you know one way or the other. But Eddie wouldn't have had that dyed-in-the-wool Protestant type of upbringing anyway but he had just never played with Catholic children – it wasn't part of his childhood.

Tensions also existed in the workplace though many young people actively worked and played to reduce them.

James Young

It must have been around '66 or '67 – round about then. I was never really aware that the troubles were progressing – I suppose a lot of people weren't aware of the progression and the split in the communities because I worked in a very mixed office; we came from all over Belfast. We went out to see James Young and he was making fun of orange jelly babies... and green jelly babies was one of his favourites and you were laughing very much at this, but with hindsight he had great insight into the split that was coming.

We were going as a complete group; we went in happy and came out happy. We laughed the whole way through; he took a poke at Catholics and they didn't take exception and he took a poke at Protestants, you know, the group that I was with didn't pick up on it – it was just comedy and just a laugh.

My mother was critically ill at the time and my head wasn't always in the office – so I had withdrawn from some of the social things and didn't realise how the social outings were starting to shrink and divisions were emerging in the office, we were still going but there wasn't the same number of outings. The manager at that time was a man from the Shankill; he brought everybody in and he said, "Right, we're going to have to do something to sort this out" so he picked out who he thought were the two antagonists on each side and sacked them. I don't know what reason he gave for it but they were dismissed.

Some of us were quite shocked and thought it was a bit over the top that these two had been made scapegoats. The rest of us just carried on working. I left then in the late '70s, so I was only there for another year but the tensions in the office weren't so bad; you still spoke. I had still a few personal friends – one girl lived in the village and the other girl lived in Ballynahinch and we would have been sort of close enough on it, and we would have still been very, very friendly so I think that's what happened, it fragmented instead of a big group coming out we went out in smaller groups.

This woman recalls the idealism of the time and her, and her friend's efforts, to build bridges.

Naked Sectarianism

It was one of those after school clubs and there was a peace conference at Corrymeela and we went, some girls from the lower sixth went to this conference and it was great as we were meeting young people who were the same age as ourselves from all over Northern Ireland and from Catholic and Protestant backgrounds. It was a nice place to meet people as well. We were all young and idealistic and some of us thought, "Right, rather than let this be just a one - off, why don't we continue to have contact with each other?" Because it's good to do that and to show that we're not so different in things that we care about like music and films and the grand debates and what it's all about. We didn't seem that different in what we were concerned about.

We established an organisation called Contact and that first Christmas we wanted to invite some of the Catholic boys' schools along to the school dance and the head teacher said she would have to think about it and discuss it with the board of governors. The decision was that the board and she didn't feel it was appropriate and it could lead to people getting themselves into dangerous situations. Well, at the time I wouldn't have understood what it would have been like to ask the school to take a policy decision on such a thing. I just felt it was pure prejudice and why should the school decide who we could meet and we could meet people outside of school and nobody could stop us and what message did it send out? That we were only allowed to meet Protestants? But I can see now that it wasn't black and white like that for the adults involved but as a seventeen year old, it struck me as naked sectarianism.

This woman recalls the Springfield Road as it was in the 1960's with great fondness. She also remembers the division and separation that was to follow, though she strove to ensure that it had only a limited impact on how she lived her life.

Springfield Road

When I first moved into that house the Springfield Road was lovely; there were plenty of shops in it, a post office in it and it was always a lovely place with the trees and all. It was a lovely place – you could walk anywhere then. You weren't afraid to walk because at that time Protestants and Catholics lived on the Springfield Road and Woodvale. But when the troubles started, while I was never afraid to walk on it, I would have been more fearful of men walking on it or your children. My children went to Springfield Road School but when they got older they probably wouldn't have went onto the road when the Troubles started. I always found that the people on both sides were always nice and everybody talked to each other. But when the Co-op and the Post Office closed it separated people because people would have met at the shops and everybody talked. One by one the shops just went and that is when everybody started getting isolated. People who were Catholic would have went mostly to the Falls Road and the lower Springfield Road whereas people on the other side would have went to the Woodvale side and on to the Shankill Road. I think they need to bring something like that back again.

I worked in the Blackstaff Mill from the 1970's to about 1989. They closed the mill down. I was a stitcher. I liked it there and I liked the people and when I went down the Springfield Road everybody would have said good morning to me. I never had any problem with it; through the Troubles and all. Even with rubble on the ground, maybe there had been riots the night before but I never got any bother.

We never had any problem in work; everybody just got on. We all had to work for a living so anybody's problems were everybody's problem. I remember one girl and she was a catholic. She was from Suffolk I think it was and she used to say to me, "Sorry, I've swore – I must put a penny in the box." You know, she respected it, she said, "I know you don't swear" and she did show respect. I used to laugh – I used to say, "I'm not worrying" but she said she had to put money in the box. There used to be a wee box and every time somebody swore they put money into it for charity. The respect was there and I knew how they lived their lives and I would have said, "It doesn't matter."

I was going down the road one day, for instance and there were young fellows on the road and they were walking up and the army stopped them and put them all against the wall. The fellows had nothing – they weren't doing anything. I could see the thing from both sides because my son was taken off the bus one morning on the Shankill because he was black-haired and he had a beard – he grew a beard at this time – and they thought he was Gerry Adams. It was half-six in the morning and he was going to work and they took him off the bus and they took him to the station so I knew what it was like with my own. So it wasn't just one-sided. I could understand how these young fellows felt and how they did make them turn against the police, because it wasn't just the one side because my sons went through it too. If they stopped to talk at a corner they were lifted but it wasn't a one-sided thing; it was on both sides. So I could understand how the parents felt with their family.

As the decade came to an end and violence accompanied civil rights protests and counter-protests the army moved on to the streets of Derry on 14th August 1969 to support a worn out and demoralized police force. The introduction of troops was seen as a 'limited operation' to restore law and order. The troops were to remain and by the mid 70's 30,000 were deployed across Northern Ireland. It was events such as the burning of Bombay Street that prompted the initial introduction of troops on to the streets of Belfast.

The world had turned upside down

I went to school at St. John's Primary School, just off the Springfield Road, and so I would have spent an enormous amount of time in my grandmothers – it was my aunt and my grandmother and then I remember coming up to '69. There are more vague memories before that. Things like Mackie's men coming up the Kashmir Road and you always had to run in and I would run in and run up the stairs and look out the window. My romantic memories of it – it was like a big grey cloud coming down the hill and there was such a profound noise of all these feet marching down.

We ran in. I suppose it was like the old fashioned Bogie men because they were all going to the Shankill so they weren't one of us, so it was like, "Mackie's men will take you away". Come five o' clock the horn would go and every child would be trailed in off the street for Mackie's men to go through the bottom of Clonard there and up onto the Shankill.

My mum had lived in Bantry Street off the Falls Road and she had just moved house up into Andersonstown – up into Ladybrook. But I was still going to school and my sister was still going to school in St. John's, so I suppose what I remember next is that we all ended up in my mummy's – my uncle, two aunts, a couple of neighbours and my mum's house being full of people. The next day, we went down to Bombay Street, to see the house. We all walked down, I was about 10 or 11 and I remember thinking that the whole world was burning. That's my strongest memory – that the whole world was on fire. My dad had a car and we parked the car in Dunville Park and walked up the Kashmir Road – or Clonard Street – and down. There were cars burning and the whole street was on fire and people wandering up and down in bewilderment of it all. For me, after that was a sort of comforting sort of time because my mum's house was full of people. There were people on mattresses everywhere.

My dad had heard the night before that there was something up. My dad would have had friends on both sides of the divide – he was called Tommy and his father was English so he could play lots of different corners and so I think he would have had people who would have told him or warned him off. So, the night before, my grandmother and my aunt and all of us – everybody had moved up to mummy's house.

The house was vacant and we'd all moved out, but we were left with nothing as we thought that maybe we'd have our windows put in or something like that; not being left with nothing.

To be a young child at that time, I can't remember the precise expression you used, but you thought that the world had turned upside down. Sometimes it all comes back to you; all that you lost in the house.

Across the city families were forced from their houses as the sectarian conflict intensified, others retreated from areas in which they were the minority, into the relative safety of what became their own communities, be they Catholic or Protestant.

Put Out

We got put out of our house, like hundreds of other people. When I went into work the next day, a lady had told her daughter to bring us to their house if we'd nowhere to stay and they lived in the middle of the Shankill. So she had offered to take us in. She was a marvellous woman as was her daughter.

We were some of the last people to leave- the last Catholic families. Our windows were broken every Saturday night and it got to the point where we just kept our sitting-room window boarded up. Then we were threatened.

Strange enough, in those early days, when big sections of the community were all moving, there was, well now you can go to the Housing Executive and say you've been intimidated and they'll give you another house. There wasn't that then; people didn't even expect help, they just tried to move on. What happened was, people getting put out of one area moved into another area where other people had been put out of.

My aunt had been in the process of buying a house in an area where most of the Protestants had been put out of on the Grosvenor Road and we moved in there; she gave up the house and we moved in there.

It is estimated that some 60,000 people were forced to move house in the early stages of the Troubles as segregation increased and people felt safer living amongst people they called their own.

On the Wrong Side of the Road

I lived in Morris Street, facing Woodvale Avenue. When the Whiterock Parade came up the Springfield we all sat on this one big step with our crisps and watched the parade. But when the Troubles started the army was there and they blocked us in. They would not let us out to see the parade because they thought we were Catholics. My Daddy went to the soldiers to say these kids always watch the bands here and they told my Daddy if he wouldn't move away they would arrest him. That was the end of the parades and the 11th night for us. And as the Troubles got worse at night we were sleeping in the church hall at Springfield Methodist. There was a lot of trouble on the road, rioting, and we moved to be safe. My Daddy put the wardrobes in front of the windows and stayed in the house. We were in the church. Everybody was sleeping there, Catholics and Protestants. There was one guy in particular. He put his car in behind the gates. As we were leaving for school in the morning he threw a bucket of water round us. He slept in the hall with us that night and the next morning he soaked us. We had to get the bus to Glencairn School on the Springfield Road; it brought us up round the West Circular. He told us, that pathway is green white and gold, don't be walking on it. We didn't understand. We didn't know anything different.

Moved Out

They came to the house with baseball bats. Then the army came down and said you would have to move out. My Mummy left the house that she had been brought up in, it broke her heart. And then we had nowhere to go. We got a house in Highfield. This man came round and said there are houses in Highfield that Catholics had moved out of and we could move in temporarily. So we got one of those. But it was awful. All we had was the clothes we stood in and what we could lift, because anything we left in the house they took out and burnt it. The people who lived beside us who we thought were our friends; there were two of them with the baseball bats. We lost all our school books, our photographs. But it was worse for our Mummy. She had lost her home, everything that she had put into it.

The welcome for the British soldiers from the Catholic community was perhaps not as universally warm as tends to be reported. They were both arriving as defenders of a beleaguered community and as representatives of what was seen by many as an occupying force. By 1974 250 British soldiers were killed during the ongoing conflict. The response to the sectarian violence in Belfast was the introduction of British soldiers on to the streets in August 1969.

Soldiers

I remember there being great talk in the family when the soldiers came – one side of my family had a quite staunchly republican background from the 20's and my father grew up in Hong Kong with delusions of grandeur – but there would have been a lot of talk about people who welcomed soldiers in and there was one particular neighbour they talked about who had her photograph taken on this soldier's knee and it was like, "Gasp! How could she?" because it was still considered by my grandparents that they were the enemy and had been for hundreds of years.

I think there were some people in the area that welcomed the soldiers but it was definitely the minority. We were told that, here they were back again – the English – and you couldn't look sideways. I remember as a young woman I suppose – you know, when you're 15, 16 or 17 – I remember looking at them, and feeling desperately sorry for them because some of them looked the same age as me.

The Soldiers

I was twelve when I first saw the soldiers. I think they came along on the streets on the 14th of August or something like that. It was 1969. I lived in Crocus Street, two streets away from it and I remember there were barricades up at the time, because a few weeks before it Bombay Street was burnt down and I remember people saying the soldiers were coming onto the streets. I and my brother and a few other wee lads who we played football with went up to the top of the street and we saw these soldiers walking up. You hear the... I think you called it whippets at the time and there were maybe a hundred or so just marching up the street and the Major or whoever it was calling out all the orders. That was scary. I thought it was frightening because the Major or whoever it was, was calling out the orders and the soldiers were turning around and actually facing you. I'd never even seen things like this in television; and this was real life just standing facing me.

The very first time I seen them, the grown-ups welcomed them, because the grown-ups thought that it was just a matter of time before other streets

were burnt out and the Catholic people at the time thought that the soldiers were here to protect them. I remember people used to bring them cups of tea and that.

I just kept away from them. Some kids – people younger, maybe 6 or 7 year-olds would have went up to the soldiers, but I didn't go near any of them. I was more-or-less scared of them. And when they did come in, I'm not too sure, you seen their berets and all – and their guns. I think it was the Paratroopers or something like that. My father, as he fought in the war, he was more-or-less welcoming of them too; he was able to tell you what regiment and all they were from. That type of thing. But definitely on the Falls Road they were welcomed for the first time.

For this woman, now living in Belfast, her memory of the appearance of soldiers on the streets of her native city, Derry, was to stay with her.

Snow in Derry

I was home from working in Zambia and it happened to be the winter months and it was just before Christmas and I'm walking up Carlisle Road in Derry. There was a soldier on patrol. As I'm going through the checkpoint this little soldier says to me "Would you ever say a prayer that we don't get any snow or rain around Christmas this year", I said, "I'm very sorry. I've worked in

Zambia for three years and I've been dying to see snow, so I've been praying we'll get snow." Sure enough we got snow that Christmas. Everybody had to put up with the snow in the street. Maybe I was very selfish, I don't know. You know in a way... you've got the sunshine all the time and the heat in a country and then you're just looking forward to some of your normal atmosphere and climate.

CHAPTER 2
1970s

Backdrop – Dancing on the Maidstone – The Falls Curfew – I'm a Wee Girl - You just carried on – You went on with your business – People just went back to work – Ormeau House – When I started to cry – Marry a Nurse – Do You Know What He is? – Living in London – Catholic Neighbours –Working in Gallaghers – Falls Burning – Gun Battle – Caravanning–Faint! Faint! – Scottish Soldiers – Everybody was on edge – House Searches – Road Blocks – ID – Security Checks – Abercorn Bomb – Springfield Methodist – Europa Hotel – 'I'm Frankie Murphy' – Christmas Cake – A bottle of sherry – UWC strike – Petrol Bombs – First Aiders – Springfield Road Bomb – Community Entertainment – Working Relations – Signs and Symbols.

Backdrop: The 'Me Decade'

The hope and optimism of the 60's, fuelled by economic prosperity, ran out of steam in the 70's. Tom Wolf labelled the decade the 'Me Decade'. Social activism and the demand for social and political change gave way to a more selfish focus on self-improvement. The music of protest was replaced by disco.

The oil crisis and the end to a long period of growth in the American economy brought recession. In Britain the Wilson administration imposed a 3 day week to conserve electricity. Television companies were required to cease broadcasting at 10.30 pm during the crisis. Britain and Ireland both joined the European Economic Community in 1973. This was to transform the Southern economy, moving it from a focus on agriculture to a high tech, export driven economy, and bring the British and Irish governments closer together, despite continuing disagreements over the North.

The Munich Massacre, in which eleven members of the Israeli team were killed, marred the 1972 summer Olympics. Israel defeated a coalition of Arab states, led by Egypt and Syria in the 1973 Arab-Israeli War, the outcome of which continues to shape relationships in the Middle East. In an echo of the North of Ireland the name of the war is itself a contested issue being variously described at the Yom Kippur War, Ramadan War or October War. Nixon, in 1972, became the first US president to visit China. Two years later he resigned, following Watergate which involved the bugging of the Democrat Party's headquarters, and the subsequent cover –up. The decade ended with the Iranian Revolution in which the deposed Shah was replaced by the revolution's spiritual leader, the Ayatollah Khomeini and the Soviet occupation of Afghanistan. Economic decline and an energy crisis shifted politics in the West to the right. Margaret Thatcher was elected British Prime Minister in 1979, a development that was to have a major impact on events in Northern Ireland.

The 70's in Northern Ireland began with troops on the streets. The troops were under the control of the Unionist administration. The initial honeymoon period, during which the troops were welcomed by the Nationalist population, eroded first with the Falls curfew in July 1970 and then, decisively, with the introduction of internment in August 1971. Between the 9th and 11th August 11 people in Ballymurphy were shot dead by members of the Paratroop regiment during the operation to introduce internment.

The republican movement split and the newly formed Provisional IRA, which had grown out to of the defence of Catholic areas in 1969, launched a bombing campaign designed to undermine the Unionist regime and force British withdrawal. The UDA, formed from the local defence organizations in Protestant areas, quickly became the largest of the Loyalist paramilitary grouping. Together with the UVF, the UDA engaged in a campaign of killing members of the Catholic community. The early years of the 70's were the bloodiest of the Troubles. 1972 began with Bloody Sunday, continued with Bloody Friday during which the IRA detonated 22 bombs in Belfast, killing 9 people and the year ended with over 400 people dead.

This was also a time of considerable political and constitutional uncertainly. Direct Rule was introduced in 1972 in the aftermath of the Bloody Sunday killings, ending fifty years of continuous Unionist rule in Northern Ireland. From 1972 onwards serious consideration was given by the Heath and Wilson administrations to options including power sharing, repartition, an independent Northern Ireland and British withdrawal. The extent of the instability led to concern that a complete breakdown of law and order was a real possibility. The 'doomsday' scenario. The search for political compromise floundered, first with the imposition of direct rule in 1972 and then with the Ulster Worker's Council Strike of 1974 and the end of the power sharing executive. The Sunningdale Agreement had delivered a short lived power sharing executive led by Brian Faulkner and foundered on the rocks of loyalist opposition to the Council of Ireland, a modest set of cross border arrangements. Seamus Mallon was later to memorably refer to the 1998 Good Friday Agreement as 'Sunningdale for slow learners'.

There is a tendency to look back and see the Troubles as a period of constant violence. Whilst the threat was always present, the reality was one of peaks and troughs. The early to mid-70's were the years in which the greatest numbers of people were killed. But even within these years there were periods of intense violence, followed by lulls. In early 1970 three of the additional eight army units brought into Northern Ireland the previous year were withdrawn as the situation apparently stabilized. However, the Falls Curfew in July undermined relationships between the Catholic community in Belfast and the army. The introduction of internment in 1971, targeted solely at the Catholic community, brought a further breakdown in relationships and a sharp increase in violence and deaths. As one of the participants in the 5 Decades Project recalled, the relationship shifted dramatically from tea and biscuits for the squaddies to graffiti proclaiming 'No tea for Dad's Army'.

Loyalist opposition to Sunningdale led again to an increase in violence and deaths. During the Ulster Workers Council strike, four car bombs exploded in Dublin and Monaghan, killing 33 people. The IRA, in the midst of a series of secret talks with the British government, called a ceasefire in late 1974. The ceasefire continued until January 1976 with a number of significant breaches during the period. But during this period there was widespread sectarian violence. The most notorious killings were carried out by the Shankill Butchers, a UVF gang under the leadership of Lenny Murphy, who were responsible for 23 deaths. In 1978 the IRA bombing of the La Mon hotel on the outskirts of Belfast resulted in twelve deaths and many severe injuries caused by the incendiary bomb.

Throughout the decade political relationships were poor. Direct rule soured relations between Unionists and the British government. Many Unionists viewed Nationalist politicians as people who, under the guise of a civil rights campaign, sought to bring down the Northern Ireland state. Nationalists considered Unionist opposition to power sharing as little more than a desire to re-impose the discredited Stormont regime. Within Unionism and Nationalism there were ongoing divisions and suspicions. The Reverend Ian Paisley was a constant critic of reformist Unionism and the SDLP, formed in 1970, was characterised by internal divisions between those who emphasised a left wing agenda within a Northern Ireland context and those who offered an all – Ireland perspective. Although natural allies of the SDLP, the Irish government, fearing the prospect of British withdrawal, refused to support SDLP calls for an end to British support for the union whilst engaging in secret contingency plans to cater for up to 50,000 Catholic refugees from the North.[8] The SDLP feared the political growth of Sinn Féin, were critical of British government contact with the IRA and were prepared to support a security crackdown against the IRA.

8 Kerr, M The Destructors, p.311

William Whitelaw, as Secretary of State, had created a sense of purpose and direction during his period of office, earning the unlikely plaudit from IRA leader, Séan MacStiofáin, that he was the only Englishman ever to pronounce his name correctly. Merlyn Rees presided over a more chaotic regime. In the words of one senior official the British government had no policy on Northern Ireland in 1975 'other than to survive for another week or fortnight'.[9] Rees was replaced by Roy Mason who announced that 'Ulster had enough of initiatives' and proceeded to focus on security, increasing covert army tactics and extending the policy of Ulsterisation which emphasised the role of the RUC and UDR and sought to criminalize the conflict. Writing in the Daily Telegraph on the occasion of Roy Mason's eightieth birthday, Geoffrey Wheatcroft refereed to Mason as 'the best Secretary of State for Northern Ireland we ever had'.[10] A view not necessarily shared by everyone.

As it became clear that the introduction of troops in the summer of 1969 was far from a temporary measure the normal infrastructure to accommodate an army developed. Soldiers moved into barracks across Belfast. Recreation was provided for soldiers when off duty.

Dancing on the Maidstone

Palace Barracks was a Wednesday night and a Sunday night. Kinnegar was a Thursday and a Saturday. They're both near Holywood. Kinnegar's was round near the sea front and Palace is just on the main road. It used to be hard to get into Palace; they used to take your photograph and all and have a wee ID card, but you still had to sign in. We also went to the Maidstone.

It was a big boat, well a ship or whatever you would like to call it. I think there was nine of us and you went down... you either got a taxi down to Dee street or we would have walked down and then when you got into Dee Street, you used to get into a big three-tonner and they'd have taken you round to the ship. There you had to sign in your name. You had all the music of the day. My friend Esther had a big black fellow called Martin and he used to put on music for us; all Motown – Diana Ross, The Supremes and things like that – and T-Rex, Slade. So it was a wee bit of everything; you'd have got up and had a laugh.

We didn't really fight over any of them; we only went to have fun with the dancing and carry on. There was enough trouble and nonsense going on without starting that in there. But if you fought you got barred anyway. You

9 Kerr p. 312
10 Daily Telegraph, 18th April 2004

weren't allowed back for so many weeks. If they'd said you were barred for four weeks, you were barred for four weeks so we didn't get up to anything.

Some of them were such a laugh and we'd have great wee nights and other times it wasn't as good as usual. You just have to take it as it comes. I even met up with a couple of girls from the Falls one night – because I wasn't allowed to go into one of the discos- and these other two girls weren't allowed to go in either. So we went outside and your man had got us a taxi back to Dee Street and she says to me, do you know where there are any other discos? I says, 'Aye', and when we were sitting in the car she asks me where I'm from. I said I'm from the Shankill and I asked where they came from, they replied the Falls. Here's me, right, okay. And I said, ' I know where there's another disco if you want to go, they agreed and so I introduced them to Kinnegar and we went. But see coming home that night... they came home that night and it was so different for me because I was going through all these areas that I didn't know but fair play to those two wee girls, they got me home that night safe onto the Shankill.

Sometimes we walked home from Holywood. Tell us about it when you're wearing high-heels too. So we've walked home many a night. But right enough they met up with us a couple of times and got on alright with them. And here she was, 'Are you going to come next week'? I said 'Aye, I'll be here next week'. Because, they said, we won't know anybody. I said, 'Sure that's alright, sure you'll know me. And I'll have my chums with me'. You see Catholic ones didn't go as much as Protestant ones – I don't know why. I think they had more of an issue with the army than the Protestant people did.

Life became increasingly difficult as relationships with the army deteriorated and violence and the threat of violence increased. A key moment in the deteriorating relationship between the Catholic community and the army was the Falls Curfew.

The Falls Curfew

I lived in West Belfast during the entire period of the troubles and I still live there. I remember a particular incident that happened during the early years of the troubles. It took place on the Falls Road in July 1970.

I belonged to a First Aid Unit called The Order of Malta. One night I was on first aid duty in St. Paul's in Hawthorn Street. My colleague and friend Anna and I were there every night from 6.00pm to 12.00pm since the start of the Troubles in 1969. We had run out of the antiseptic liquid Savlon which

we used for treating injuries so I said to Anna that I would go home, have something to eat, and then go down to another First Aid post in Sultan Street and get some Savlon and I arranged to meet her in St. Paul's Hall at 7.30 pm.

I never did get to St. Paul's Hall that night. The British Army had put one side of the Falls Road on curfew which meant it also included Sultan Street with me still inside the First Aid Post. Nobody knew where I was the whole night except Anna. We were not allowed out or even to open the door. The head man of the First Aid unit was also there, a Dr. McAllister. He went to open one of the doors and one of the British soldiers shouted at him 'Close the fucking door!' Then I could smell the C.S gas they were firing. We listened to gunfire and rubber bullets being fired for most of the night and we could do nothing to help anyone who was injured.

We were held in the hall the whole night and most of the next day. The only way out was when the brave women from Andersonstown marched down the Falls Road and broke the curfew. What a sight it was! Hundreds of women, some of them pushing prams and bringing us food and water, pushing the British Army aside to break the curfew and get us free. I will never forget those brave Irish women and the stand they took that day against the British Army. I will always remember The Falls Road Curfew.

As the North of Ireland descended into violence and chaos, lives were altered and destroyed

I'm a wee girl

I lived on the Shore Road. I had four sisters and two brothers and mommy and daddy in a two bedroom bungalow. They were pulling them down so we moved to Ballymurphy. When we lived on the Shore Road it was always a mixed community, so we never really felt any different. We went to Ballymurphy and it was still the same – never really thought anything of it. It wasn't really a republican family. My father came from Monaghan but outside of that – that was as much Republican as we really knew, which would be none whatsoever.

When the Troubles started it was a big shock in a sense because we didn't really understand it. I remember being fascinated by all these names you never heard before like 'internment'. I remember being petrified of Paisley; he was supposed to be saying to send all the Catholics down to the South of Ireland to live. What struck me more was when the people were burnt out in '69 of the Lower Falls and they were brought up to St. Thomas' school. Me and my friends would go down and help the children and play with them. It was like we were on our summer holidays – you didn't see the seriousness in it or the bad end of it. There wasn't as much press, you had TV but you were kids you never watched the news or anything. You didn't really understand although I had older brothers and sisters.

When internment came it brought it into reality with my mommy being killed. It's just that fear that you had when all those people were being shot. I remember one day coming up Ballymurphy Road and it was the evening, it was dark, it was about 6 o'clock, and this voice from the entry calling me up. I realised it was the English voice and I was panicked and shouted 'I'm a wee girl, I'm a wee girl' and he said 'it doesn't matter come up'. This neighbour come up and said 'what are you playing at, isn't it bad enough you killed that girl's mother without annoying her'. I felt like saying 'shut up mister, don't be telling them my mommy's dead because then they'd be thinking she's a bad one and I'm a bad one and panic freaked me out. He gave off that much and he refused to let me go up the entry and he put me on up the street. I lived in fear of him coming to knock the door because they said my mommy was an IRA woman but she was a completely innocent woman. If they thought she was a gunwoman they might think I was helping her. You're so young, you're only 14 and you're thinking this is so terrible.

In those times it was so frightening. You're lying in bed and you'd seen the flash in the window and you knew the bomb was coming next and shooting and army banging in doors. It just was so frightening and your mommy wasn't there and your mommy was your saviour and your mommy kept you safe and you lost all that. Even going to the dentist I was terrified because she wasn't there. I married in '75 and had a child in '75. When you look back you were having a child of your own and you are only a child. I turned 18 in June and was married in August. We lived at home for a year and then got a place of your own. I always think you turned into an old woman overnight. It was so frightening. You were responsible for this child when your husband went to work and you were petrified he wasn't coming back.

And in the midst of pain and suffering ordinary people sought to live their lives, to 'carry on', to go about their business as best they could.

You just carried on

My younger sister, the year after my mommy was killed, she was standing dancing in the next street – her and her two friends were jiving. She was the one doing the partner, throwing these two around. The next thing there was gunfire and one friend lay dead and the other lay injured and there wasn't a mark on her. You know what I was doing – piercing my ear in the mirror with a needle and thread, when I heard the whole shooting. Somebody screamed and I run around and I remember going 'Oh my God'. Then the ambulance came – they never even took her to the hospital. My daddy brought her down just to see her friend. She was never going for claims or saying I was there or anything. Her wee friend died and she was devastated but I remember going round and saying this is terrible, this is terrible and then going on out with my friends because it was classed as a normality. God love her, my daddy took her to the hospital and I remember going in and talking to her and saying aw, you'll be alright, you'll be alright. You put up this wall and you didn't let it soak in, you didn't accept it. You were carrying on as if nothing happened. That same evening I went down with my mates down in Clonard meeting up with these boys, having a laugh and a carry on. You just carried on; you never stopped to think that you weren't reacting the way you were supposed to.

I think it boiled down to the fact that when my mommy was murdered and we were sent away, when we came back there was no counselling, there was no talk. We didn't even know what happened until we started investigating into it ourselves about 20 years ago. I don't think my daddy knew what happened either. The story we were told was that my mommy was out and they fired gas and I bolted. As you can imagine I was a handful at 14. The storyline was, with the shooting this is what we were told, when the shooting started she was in a place of safety. But someone was shot and someone else was shot and she panicked and she was heard to say 'I have to get home to my kids' and they heard shooting and they heard her screaming that she was blind and couldn't see, then more shooting and they never heard her again. The sister that was with us, she stayed with her but she has no memory of that day.

You went on with your business

I remember one day walking down Leeson Street and kids were rioting and throwing stones at the army. I wasn't even married at the time; this was 1972 or '73 maybe. Next thing this nail bomb came over the roofs of the houses. Me and my friend run and we got into this house in time. We were just shaking and we couldn't believe we had just escaped getting blown up. You went on with your business. Me and my friend went round and had a cup of tea and you just went on with it.

People just went back to work

I worked in town so you got searched regularly – even from one shop to the next and then after a while it just became automatic and I can remember going to London and going into the shop and doing that with my handbag and people looking at me. It got to the point where you never thought anything of it; you just walked in and opened your bag and I think that was very, very telling and I also worked there during a lot of the bombing. So you were going into the city centre and the bombs were going off around you and you just had to keep going; it was amazing people just went back to work the next day or went back to work that afternoon.

They were so commonplace, but I remember walking down the street on a summer's day – I was going to my mother-in-laws at the time, it was a beautiful summer's day with children playing football and the next thing – oh the bang! And this child was standing with no clothes on and his shoes were lying all over and his hand was blown off... his hand was hanging off... just in a split second... somebody had put a bomb under his dad's car. The ball had went under and he went to get it and it was a really, really horrific and for all the things you hear and all the things that have happened since that's one of my enduring memories... of this child. He would have been about eight. The family still lived there, he grew up but he did lose his hand, but the family didn't move – they just stayed and carried on.

And although people carried on the potential for violence to disrupt the pattern of everyday life was an ever present possibility.

Ormeau House

My sister and I had snuck out one night to go up to a céilidh and we had come in quite late, managed to get in and as we were starting to undress when a bomb went off, just opposite our house, and all our windows got blown in and the panic that we were in was – our dad's going to come in and find out we were out – this bomb took second place to this. But that was our big worry, would we got caught.

Our Dad was running round... you know there were eight of us – so he was actually going round rooms to make sure everybody was alright. So he probably opened the doors and asked if everybody was alright and then carried on to the next room.

It was Ormeau House that was blown up. It used to be the old register – births and marriages. So it was a government building that had been blown up... but it didn't do a lot of damage because the building is still there.

For this woman the work environment was hostile and extremely difficult. Much campaigning and fair employment legislation, beginning with the Fair Employment Act of 1976, was to bring change but the price was paid by the workers who had to endure bullying, harassment and violence. Yet this woman managed to find a way through it all.

Working in Gallagher's

I started work in Gallagher's in 1969. Then they didn't employ very many Catholics so I thought I was dead lucky getting in. My elder sister had worked in it years before but there were no Troubles on then. So whenever I got started I was all delighted – great job, great to their staff, great money, bonuses twice a year. You got a big one in July – but that was like themed on the Protestants. And the next one was Christmas. I was happy as Larry; I had many, many Protestant friends. When it came to the Twelfth they stopped talking to you for about fortnight but then they liked you again after that, after the Twelfth was over. Thursday the 23rd of September 1971 it just was an ordinary day to me; I went to work as usual. The night before me and my boyfriend went to his sister's house in Abercorn Street just for a wee yarn and we were writing our wedding lists, guest lists, we was getting married, we were saving up, so we didn't go out much.

Jim's brother and his girlfriend had left bomb making material in Marion Street and that wasn't to be touched again. But houses were very hard to get in them days and this woman heard of the empty house and her and her family wanted to move into it. So a fella came up to him and said the woman was going to move in, he couldn't possibly allow them because of the bomb making material. So he came down to Abercorn Street and he couldn't get in touch with his girlfriend so he came in and asked me to go with him. He said, 'would you wheel the pram around with me and we'll move the stuff as if we're just a wee married couple' so it wouldn't have looked suspicious. I was nearly going to go with him, when his girlfriend turned the corner and he said 'it's OK; go on you back to our Jim'. She took over and they went around. They said after the death it was a case of misadventure, it was a ring or something around their neck that triggered the bomb off and the two of them got killed. So I was away home all that night, we heard on the news that two people were killed on the Lower Falls but I never thought in a million years it was anything to do with me.

I went into work the next morning as usual and my own work mates used to cheer and they'd say 'another two of your ones blew up last night'. I used to go on about my business never thinking. I didn't know until lunch time. Jim's mommy was going into the hospital to have an ulcer removed. Every year that she was supposed to go in she was pregnant and it went on and on and on until she got old. So I got out of work, finished half day in Gallagher's, and went away around to British Home Stores and got her a wee nighty and dressing gown for the hospital and I was going up to her house that night. So I went on and wasted a bit of time when I think about it, shopping in the town. When I got on up to my own house my mommy and daddy said you have to go down to hers, that was Jim's brother, that was killed last night. I, for some reason, walked it up Ballymurphy and got the Springfield Road bus down, away out of my own way, instead of going down the Whiterock Road. Anyway that was the Friday, he got killed on the Thursday, I was at work on Friday, Saturday and Sunday were my days off, the funeral was Monday so I didn't go into work. I phoned and said I wouldn't be in; you had to let them know. I went back into work on Tuesday. That's where it started, that's when my career in Gallagher's ended.

The boss said 'what was wrong with you yesterday?'. I said 'my future brother-in-law died and I was at the funeral'. He said, 'I seen it on the news. If I had it my way he'd be hanging from them rafters'. All my workmates, all the people I thought liked me and knew me as a person beforehand refused to work with me. That was September. I got my tea on my own, they wouldn't drink out of the same cup as me. I went on my lunch on my own. The management came and said for your own safety you're going to have to sit in the cloak room every day, don't come up onto the floor. They probably thought I would've said oh, I'm leaving. But I was as bitter as all them and I said it'll do me if I'm getting paid and I'm sitting in the cloak room every day.

One of the days the shop steward, she was a small wiry woman, she was coming towards me and the closer she got I thought she was going to hit me. She pushed me down to the ground and lay on top of me so they stabbed her. She seen them coming behind me to get me but I could see her coming towards me, by the look on her face I thought my God she's going to do something on me. She just pushed me down, she was a wee wiry thing, and lay on top of me and they stabbed her. By that time that was all the commotion over. We all worked with half-moon knives to cut your tobacco with. We had our own mini hospital because people had lost arms and all in the big machinery. They took her down to the sick bay. She was back down on the floor in no time with her arm strapped up. I went to the boss and I told him what happened and he said send for the shop steward. And when she came in I said, 'tell him what happened'. She said, 'no I fell'. I said send for the nurse who fixed her up. The nurse came and I said 'tell the management what you dressed, what you done to her when she was hurt' and she said 'oh no, she fell and I just strapped her arm up'. I hadn't a leg to stand on. After that, when they knew they were going to get me on the floor with weapons then I was reduced to sitting in the cloak room.

Whenever you arrived to go in the gate of Gallagher's there was random searches coming in. There was a fella and he made my life hell. He just used to call me 'Ballymurphy'. Whenever we were rolling in he'd say, 'here's Ballymurphy, make sure you search her she's not carrying anything in'. They searched me more often than they searched anyone else. He thought it would have annoyed me and got me in trouble but I just sort of got used to it. In them days the girls came to work with rollers in their hair and a scarf tied around it. You were allowed to smoke as many cigarettes a day as you wanted but you weren't allowed to take any out. They used to put them in their rollers. They weren't stamped so that's how they knew that they were from the factory floor.

You had to get a pass out to make a phone call. I had a safe house number and name in the New Lodge if I ever was in real danger that my daddy had given me to get in touch with these people. Some of the other one's would have said, they're on the war path today, you know the Protestants, so they were half warning me that something was going to happen. I got in the lift, the hoist it was a big, big hoist. As you can imagine there was trolleys of tobacco and everything going into it. It was bright and cheery on the floor and you took your turn and you were allowed to pick the records for the week. A whole lot of them, their boyfriends were either sailors or soldiers, and they used to play 'Sailors stop your roaming' and we'd look over at each other and 'that one's for you Valerie' and 'that one's for you'. Good days. Oh good, good days. Good to their staff and good wages then, what we must've been earning the men at the shipyard wouldn't have been earning.

I got into the lift and that fella who made my life hell got in with his mate and he put a knife to my throat. I don't really think he would've used it. How would they have accounted for that, for me going missing? The history behind me, the management knew I was sort of a risk. Whenever they stopped it between floors I rolled out and dropped down to get onto safe ground. When I used to go home and tell these hairy stories at home our ones used to be raging.

I clocked in in the morning, sat there, was allowed up on the floor to have my tea break, my lunch, and my afternoon tea break. You were bored to tears, but I wouldn't leave and I was getting my wages at the end of the week. My daddy and mommy and husband to be were all distracted. They were saying 'you better get out of there and you better leave and all'. We were getting married on the 5th February. Jim's brother died in September so that went right on like that and then in January I was in work that day and I came home and mommy said 'your cards came in the post today, you were paid off for bad timekeeping'. There was no unfair dismissal in them days. The more I think about it, even talking about it now, I wasn't at my post for a month or so. So I wasn't working, I was sitting in the cloak room. They might have got me that way and said 'but sure you haven't been on the floor'.

We were getting married in a couple weeks and I had no job where before I had a healthy salary. Jim worked in Musgrave Park Hospital. But he used to go on a wee bike up the Falls, down Stockmans, cut through the park and out into Musgrave. But then the soldiers were based there so then they used to say to him, 'we're watching you, we know exactly what way you come to work, we're going to get you. First your brother and now you.' And then they were writing in the toilets about him, 'You're next', his own workmates that were Protestants so it was better if he left. That was the two of us out of work, getting married in the next week. When I think about it, I suppose Jim might have, not made me leave, but once we were married he would've had a say in the matter. And my mommy and daddy said you're going to lose your religion, you're going to get killed if you don't get out of there.

After I'd had Nuala I'd had a lump and I was in the Royal getting it removed in 1972. This girl was in the bed facing me and we got talking 'what are you in for' and all. When I said I worked in Gallagher's she said 'Oh, my brother worked in Gallagher's' I said, 'what do you call him, maybe I knew him?' It was him. He came in that night to visit her. My husband was late, he had to see to the child before he come up to me. I was watching her and whenever he came into visit her she must've said 'that girl over in the bed there used to work in Gallagher's' and whenever he looked over he turns and sees and run. As he was running out of the ward, Jim was coming in. They had bypassed each other you know. I was frantic and I was saying to Jim 'that's him, that's the one who gave me all the trouble'. He went out the corridor after him and he was away thank God, if Jim had a got him.

Isn't it a small world like me meeting that girl and she was saying, 'my brother works there and all'. I would see him on the road yet. He must have to go to the hospital himself for some kind of treatment. He always sits at the bus stop on the Falls Road and he looks at you and looks away. I wouldn't challenge him now. I'd never forget but I'll never forgive them. Imagine a young girl at 16 starting off in life, I thought the older one would've helped you and all. They must have just done what their bosses did, led by the pack you know, that kind of way. I still see different ones. I used to go to bingo on North Street when mommy was still alive, that was like the foot of the Shankill, and people would come in and they'd say 'I know your face' and I'd say 'no, I work at the Royal'. Different girls you would've worked with. Some of the girls were as bad as the fellas, but then so was I. I was bitter too; I could've left if I'd have wanted to. But I thought why put you out of your bread and butter? I was thinking of me and Jim getting a wee house and starting off life like and that was the two of us on the brew. It was the one and only time. That was January. I started working at the Royal, it was supposed to be holiday relief, but that was me there forever.

We were married in '72 and I got a job starting in the Royal Hospital which was closer to home. I stayed there for 25 years, brilliant, ended up an auxiliary nurse. Jim got in as a porter and he stayed for 30 years. Indirectly all that, I don't mean it done me any favours, but it turned out fine.

There comes a point when carrying on is no longer possible.

When I started to cry

It was a few years ago, shortly after the death of my mother , It was a normal day and I was walking down the street when I started to cry, I sobbed my heart out , I cried as if my heart would break and I just couldn't stop.

I managed to get home and my husband, who could do nothing to help me, took me to the doctor, it was the beginning of a complete mental breakdown. I have gone through a lot of therapy and treatment since then and I can now tell the story of how I found myself in such a state.

In 1966 I was 18 years old and engaged to my childhood sweet heart, we went to Canada on a £10 emigration ticket, intending to earn enough money to get married. I wasn't very happy there but after a year my father-in-law was killed in an industrial accident and we came home, to help not just with the funeral but to help my mother-in-law with the eight children still at home. We did get married and lived with my mother-in-law and were living there in '69 when the troubles really started. Our daughter was born in December 1969 but she was stillborn, I was not given a reason for her death. Just over a year later we had a healthy baby boy.

On the morning of internment a neighbour knocked our door and told us about the arrests so my husband went on the run. My Dad called that morning and asked me if my uncle and his family could come and stay with me for a while, because they were on an interface and didn't feel safe with the rioting. I said of course they could come, and I told him my husband was away and I hadn't had any sleep. We had just found out I was expecting again.

My Dad took the baby over to my Mummy's to let me get a sleep, he said he'd tell her the good news about the baby and he would see me later over at their house. That was the last time I ever saw my Daddy alive, he never even told my Mum about the baby. Later that day my Mum came to my house to tell me my Dad had gone to help my uncle and family move to my house and he hadn't been seen since. Because of all the arrests we started calling round the army barracks to ask if he had been arrested.

During the day there was sporadic shooting, and we heard rumours that my Dad was one of the injured. We went back to the army barracks. They sang "where's your papa gone" out of the sanger at us but didn't give us any information, we eventually got a lift to the morgue and there we identified my father's body. He had multiple gunshot wounds, witnesses later told us that he was shot in the legs and was crying out for help and trying to crawl to cover when there was another burst of shooting and he was shot in the back.

We buried my Dad from my house, my mother was in a terrible state. A few months later my husband was arrested and interned, I was helping both our mothers and pregnant, with a toddler and visiting the Kesh. When our second son was born my husband couldn't get compassionate leave. 48 hours after the birth the baby started to decline. He passed away in my arms, my husband arrived a few hours too late to see his son alive, he couldn't bear to look at him, we buried him with my father. I was not given a death certificate and didn't know why he'd died.

After 6 months my husband was released. We continued to support both families and I was working full time as a carer. I had twin brothers who were in care since they were 9 years old; they had behavioural and learning problems and were in a boy's home because of anti-social behaviour and truancy. The IRA drove up to the home and the Christian brothers released the boys to them, they were abducted, tortured and one was murdered as an informer, the other survived but was in shock, and became increasingly withdrawn and difficult , eventually we had to sign him into Muckamore for secure accommodation.

We went on to have three more healthy children. Over the years there were a number of investigations into both deaths and 30 years after his murder my brother's name was cleared and we received an apology. My mother was dying of cancer by then when I told her the good news all she said was "I always knew he was innocent, sure he didn't have the sense to be a threat to anyone".

I nursed my mother until she died, and we buried her. Through a friend I found out I could make an application to find out why my two babies died so unexpectedly, and eventually I got the death certificates and a reason for their deaths, they had a congenital heart condition, the diagnosis helped me accept their deaths.

It was shock that after all this time and following my mother's death and so much information about the events of the past that I had this mental break down, it was as if I couldn't grieve for over 30 years and at last it was safe to let out all that agony and grief and pain. I have had a lot of medication, therapy and counselling since that day and at last the future is looking a lot more promising.

Marrying a nurse

I had a cousin who was shot, he was a lovely fella. He was paralysed. He was engaged and all but his girlfriend left him, and he ended up marrying a nurse who looked after him in the hospital. I think she was from Derry. She had no children or nothing. He died after 7 or 8 years. She's married and all again. We haven't seen her since he died.

The violence contributed to increasing segregation, despite the determination of some to live beyond the sectarian boundaries.

Do You Know What He Is?

Billy married my chum. His family were real staunch Catholics. That's the way his father and mother was, everything had to go through the chapel. When he started to go with my chum his mother never knew. But someone went and told her that her son was going with a Protestant. This Saturday me and my chum were minding her granny. The door knocked. I opened the door and there was this priest standing. I shouted in the door, 'Irene, there is a priest here looking for you'. She came out to the door and he said, 'Are you Irene' and she said 'Yes', and he said, 'Do you go with a parishioner of mine, Billy'. And she said, 'That is right'. And he said his mother wants to know that if you get married are you going to convert to our faith. And she said no.

The two kept seeing each other and they got engaged. His mother did everything to try and stop it. But they got married in the City Hall. They had two children and they moved up into the Glencairn and nobody in the

Glencairn knew what he was. Irene was a wee girl that would talk to anybody, everybody was her friend. Billy had started a band and bought them uniforms and instruments and one evening Irene happened to say 'Isn't it a terrible thing that it took a Roman Catholic to start up an Orange band'. She didn't mean it to cause offense but it must have fell on sore ears. A couple of weeks later their house was robbed and all the money belonging to the band was taken and a notice put up on her door 'All taigs out'. They moved across to a Catholic neighbourhood. He was the type of fella that mixed in with anybody. It has always stuck with me, why did they do that to Billy, he started up a football club and all for the kids. The church and his Mother did everything to stop him, they sent nuns and all to Irene, but you can't stop love.

For some, predominantly single young people and young families, the response to the conflict was emigration, whether to England or to further afield, often Australia or Canada. For this young man the experience of moving away was not just about escape, it was also about opening up new opportunities.

Living in London

I was overwhelmed by not having to look behind me. It seemed like a whole new world. It wasn't just the Troubles, it was the whole thing. There were no restrictions, there was freedom. Maybe sometimes you took that a bit far, but

it was a long way from Belfast where you had to watch all the time, be careful where you went and your family, especially your mother, feared for you. It was a different way of life altogether.

For this family it was about escape, getting away from the violence and the narrow mindedness.

Catholic Neighbours

It must have been that somebody had contacted the police on the confidential phone number and suggested that they had guns buried in the garden, because the garden was dug up, the house was ransacked, the loft pulled apart and these were small, two bedroom, semi-detached houses so you could hear how horrendous it was. They were a lovely young couple but they were Catholic; he was from Ardoyne and she was from the Bone.

Well, they just decided that they had enough and didn't want to bring up a family in this kind of a place and they emigrated to Canada. It just seemed unbelievable.

All they had wanted was their children to have a better life than they had had. They were buying their wee house, you know. Sure, nothing was ever found.

Falls Burning

I think I became aware of the Troubles the night they burned the mills on the Falls. I was living on the Antrim Road. We had slept right through the night and we didn't know till we woke up when somebody said the Falls road was burning – that was the first we knew. Naturally we went over to see if our mother was alright and we saw the devastation which was awful.

She lived on the Falls, she lived just off the Grosvenor Road.

Gun Battle

The day I got out of the hospital there was another gun battle on our street. I had to climb out of the taxi on my hands and knees to get into the house after my operation. A soldier was shot that day. It was a wee kitchen house and we got a wee folding out bed and I lay there. A couple of nights after there was a hijacking of an ice cream van. Somebody opened the door and handed me a big box of ice lolly pops and set them in the bed for the kids. Half of them were thrown out because you didn't have a fridge-freezer then, but I was still lying there recovering.

For some whilst the option of moving abroad was not available, there were other escape routes. In the early days of the Troubles many families, particularly women and children, moved across the border to avoid the violence. As the conflict developed it became almost customary for children, during the heightened violence of the summer months, to be taken to England or to the United States as organizations such as Northern Ireland Children's Holiday Scheme (NICHS) emerged.

Caravan Story

It was around 1972. My sister told me that they were selling caravans in Millfield. She said a couple of people from North Belfast had bought them and they're great and she said 'You could get one for all your kids to take them out of the trouble'. I said, 'I have absolutely no money, where would I get the money for a caravan'? I knew nothing about caravans anyway, I'd never been in one, never been on a holiday in a caravan. We went down anyway to Millfield and we seen this caravan and we went inside. It was great, it was very old fashioned, gas mantles and coal fire. The guy says there were two bedrooms. You opened the door and there were two wee bunks in one of the bedrooms and the other one was a double room and there was a man sleeping in it. I said, 'Jesus does he come with the caravan'? I don't know who he was but he must've been a gypsy anyway. I thought the caravan was great and I said to the man how much is it? He says we do it for £1,000. Well that was like a million pound to me.

I went up home and I said to her that would be great for the kids, you know how you get all enthusiastic and it would be fabulous and all, but where would I get it? I was only in the credit union, but you had to have 13 weeks to get a loan. I had £13 in the credit union (and they would usually only double your money). But as the Troubles were on and people were worried about their kids anyway, I went around and says to the man, "I could buy a caravan and I could take my kids away and take them out of the Troubles" because I had at that time seven wee boys and a wee girl. I said "I'll take them somewhere", didn't know where I was going to take them like, but anyway. The long of the short of it was they gave me the money, which I couldn't believe. I went down the next day with my sister, I never even told my husband, and got the caravan. Then he got home from work and I says, "Geordie I bought a caravan". He says 'what, where are you going to put it?' I said Jesus I don't know where to put it, where would you put it? He said he worked with a fella who had a place down in County Louth at Giles Key. I had never heard of Giles Key, you might as well of said to me the United States of America. I said

"OK you get on the phone to him", everybody was running about like mad men, trying to get me somewhere to go.

Eventually Tommy said his sister lived down there and they knew the people who owned the caravan site. The caravan was still down at Millfield at this point and went I went down the gypsy man said "right we'll take you down to Giles Key". I was on my own and I had to climb up the steps of this big, big van. I didn't even know where I was going. They took me down to Giles Key. When they turned in the man who owned the caravan park said no no no, you're not getting into this caravan park. Once he seen the gypsies he thought I was a gypsy too. He says you're not getting into this caravan park. I was crying. He says it's alright, we'll get you somewhere. They turned the big van out of the park and they brought me into the beach and they sat it down on the beach and unloaded it, and they just left me on the beach. I was sitting crying right on the sandy beach. I didn't know if the tide was going to come in and wash me away or not.

It turned out OK on the beach for a while because eventually my husband came down with the kids and everyone thought it was the best thing since sliced bread. I had arms like Arnold Schwarzenegger because all I done was brush sand out. The whole day you were brushing sand, the kids were jumping in from the beach. I ended up having to wash the dishes in the sea, because there was no running water, every time I needed a new dish I had to wash it in the sea. It was a terrible time when it came to peeling potatoes because there was that many of them. There was 33 came one time, my other sister came down with her kids. There were public toilets up a bit. I couldn't peel them without running water (an old fear from the Famine). My sister used to come up with me and we'd be in the toilets and we'd lock the front door of the toilets and peel the potatoes in the running water. We had to go down to the well for water; there was a wee well up the hill. The kids absolutely loved it. I was down on the beach for six months until it came to the end of summer holidays. They lit fires outside and you'd get a bag of coal. My husband was brilliant at telling ghost stories. I never was a girl guide so I had no clue what to do. The farmer, at the end of the day, he said to me, he would take me up the hill. Well, my God, you would've thought I went to the Malone Road, just brought up the hill. Still no running water and no facilities but we stayed there for years. The kids would've went over to the farm and stacked all the hay stacks and done different things. One day a big ship came into the harbour and the kids used to go over on a dingy. My kids knew everybody and your man took them over on the dingy. I went over one day, you had to climb up on a roof ladder to get into this ship. Little did I know, it was the Marita Anne, or whatever you call it, it was a gun running ship. It wasn't a nice ship.

It was really to keep them safe. It was terrible at the times. Even when they were going to school, they used to go to the Christian brothers down beside the Sinn Féin office there. Every day, there were gun battles coming up and down. Here's me, I have to get these ones away somewhere.

I've always been lucky. I used to get lifts from there when I had to go to work on a Saturday. I left my kids there for 6 weeks. There was no badness, everybody seemed to be good.

But in Belfast danger was never far away.

Faint! Faint!

I can't really remember the year – it was the early '70s and I was out having a drink with my husband, my brother and my cousin. It was one of the wee shebeens that they had – the Cracked Cup, you called it. Somebody came in and says there's a gun battle going on out there and I says, 'I have to get home then to my children'. First I walked my brother and my cousin around to my house around the corner and then I came back to my husband to accompany him and my other cousin home. The three of us come out the second time and as we walked down Leeson Street and cut down to Balkan Street there was an army Sarasen and the next thing they called the fellas over. 'I want your identification'. Our opinion was they were using them as protection so whoever was doing the shooting wouldn't shoot at the Sarasen because they had them ones in front of them. The next thing the shooting started anyway! My husband pushed me against the wall and everybody had their front doors closed at the time. My husband says to me 'faint, faint!' so I let on to faint. He got down beside me to get away from the bullets. He says 'don't you open your eyes'. We didn't know at the time but the soldiers actually thought that I got shot because I fell. So when the battle started quieting down the soldiers asked 'is your wife injured' and he says 'I don't know' and the soldiers carried me into the Sarasen and I was lying over their knees. I had to let them carry me into the Sarasen and let on I was fainted. They brought us over to Mulhouse Street Station. This was about say half two in the morning. They kept us there until 8 o'clock in the morning. They didn't charge us or anything. We went down into the house to see the family.

This woman recalls the killing of the first off duty soldiers in Northern Ireland during the conflict. It was common at that time for television programmes, particularly late at night, to be interrupted with news bulletins or requests for key holders to attend the site of bombings.

Scottish Soldiers

I was laughing because I was watching Rowan, it must have been a Sunday night and Rowan and Martin's Laugh-In was a big, big thing – there was nothing comparable to it here and I can remember that particular night, my aunt Miriam was there... It was 1971, I think.

I know it was a long time ago, but our house was actually quite full; Eddies' granny was there and my aunt Muriel, Eddie's son and his mummy and daddy were probably there too. I can remember we had the light out as people used to switch the light off to watch television here, in the old days. I remember us all sitting... we had quite a big television at the time, it was a 26" TV; 19 was sort of the standard then. I don't know if that's why they were over or if they were just over visiting; I've no idea. But we were watching Rowan and Martin's Laugh-In and that particular night... there was an actor, I think it was Mastroianni, I'm not sure – something like that - a dark curly-haired Italian, he played some light-hearted roles in some of the films we seen him in. But he was on this show and Goldie Hawn used to be on but he [Mastroianni] had been very good and very interesting in the show, at the end of Laugh-in there was always a really silly, funny thing with which they closed the show... as I say there's this big heart-throb actor, as he was, stopping with the dark curly hair and somebody reached out and pulled his wig off and he was baldy! It was a bit of a shock but it was hilarious and we were all sitting doubled up laughing while the credits were running and they interrupted the end of the programme to make the announcement that there had been three soldiers killed over Ligoniel.

And I remember the older others telling me, as I was an awful giggler as a younger person, they were sort of telling me shut up, you know "shut up till we hear this" and they, being sort of caught up in this laughter and finding it hard just to stop laughing, and that's what it was... the three soldiers it was the strangest sensation going from being doubled up in two laughing at something to hearing the horrific news... and two of them were brothers, two brothers and a friend. So I can remember that as clearly as it was yesterday, though it was over forty years ago is it?

But it was just that very strange thing of going from hilarious laughter; it wasn't just a giggle it was like hilarious laughter. And then they broke the news

– interrupting the credits which was quite a common thing –"We interrupt this programme..." to, you know. Sometimes it was just to call key-holders back if there'd be incendiaries or something found. You know it was quite a common thing for programmes to be interrupted and I remember that very clearly and how sad it was, you know, and they were very young men, they were young fellows. It's surprising how clear a memory it still is, more than half of my life ago.

Under instructions of Brian Faulkner, the Northern Ireland Prime Minister, with the agreement of Ted Heath, the British Prime Minister, internment was introduced on 9th August 1971. During Operation Demetrius, 342 people were arrested. Despite being encouraged by Heath to take 'balancing actions' including the arrest of Loyalists, all those interned were from a Catholic or Nationalist background. During 4 days of intense violence following the introduction of internment 20 civilians, two Provisional IRA members and two British soldiers were killed.

The Morning of Internment

The soldiers came into the street before most people were up, breaking down doors and wrecking houses. I remember during the day the place was mad. People building barricades, rioting against the army. No one felt safe for days and days. There was fighting with the Protestants who were throwing petrol bombs over the wall and our one's were throwing back. And there was gunfire. Our parents tried to keep us indoors.

Belfast Telegraph

INTERNMENT

SECURITY SWOOP ON IRA SUSPECTS

300 taken for questioning in dawn swoops

There was a general sense of unease as tensions and fears increased.

Everybody Was On Edge

Everybody was on edge. We visited Castleward, it was a beautiful sunny day. We were having a picnic. An elderly man came over and challenged us, thought we were bombers because, he said, we were acting suspiciously. So even in the most innocent of settings the suspicion and unease was there.

In 1971 alone there were over 17,000 house searches, many routine rather than based on intelligence.

House Searches

The army would arrive about five thirty, six in the morning when they were doing a house search. They wouldn't have left until nine thirty, ten. You got the day off school because you couldn't get dressed when they were there. The police accompanied the army, the house would have been surrounded, everybody in the street knew. It was like a badge of honour, your house being searched. I would have went into school the next day and said 'I wasn't in yesterday, Miss, cause I got raided'. Thinking, look, aren't I so important.

This was the early 70's, feelings were very strong. We were raided quite a bit with boys in the house. The first thing drew your attention was an almighty banging on the door. One way or the other they are getting in, you are not going to stop them. So many soldiers were put round the perimeter of the house with their guns so nobody could get out of the house. The first thing they always asked 'Who's the head of the household' which is always your Daddy. He would have been told to get all of the family into the living room. We would all have been called into the living room in our pyjamas, our nightwear, whatever and if you ever had a dog, we always had a mongrel; the dogs would go bananas at the soldiers. The dog would be barking. We would be sitting along the sofa. The police came in with a piece of paper which gave them the power to do the search. So many soldiers would have been brought into the house and the police would have searched the soldiers. All the guns were put in a big canvas bags on the floor in front of the soldiers and those guns had to stay there whilst they conducted the search. My Daddy would have accompanied the army around the house, room by room, the house was searched. Sometimes they dug up the garden. What I used to hate is, I used to get it into my head, that they were all touching my underwear. It really bothered me. In a way it felt like you were getting robbed. Nothing was ever found in the house. There was never a subsequent arrest.

One time there was a small room between other bedrooms. My Daddy had decided to make home brew and all the bottles were in this spare bedroom as nobody was sleeping in it. The army had put all their guns down and were just starting to conduct the search. The soldiers were half way up the stairs when at six o'clock in the morning these beer bottles decided to explode. I remember the big scrambling match down as they thought they were being ambushed. When I remember their faces I can laugh at it but they weren't at all pleased.

Travelling to work became increasingly difficult as security measures created delays and workers themselves became potential targets of sectarian killings.

Road Blocks

Travelling from Andersonstown was the problem. When I started in Michelin, I was riding a motorbike at first and I got a car as there was an opportunity to give lads a lift from Andersonstown. Before the trouble began there was no bother, but then after that we were advised to take different routes; we could have gone up Agnes Street, Northumberland Street, round to Millfield, over by Ardoyne; different routes. The only comical thing was, with the lads I was travelling, if you said you were going to cut across the Shankill, it was a no-no. They were very frightened of that.

I came from the Shankill; so it didn't bother me, although it should have; I should have been conscious of that. There are a lot of other cases when police roadblocks, bomb scares and so on were very annoying. I remember one of the tours took us two hours, going up different routes, being turned back, and ended up going along the Shore Road towards Carrick to work our way over towards Mallusk. There was a wee man in the back complaining, "We're never going to get there, we're never going to get there" and then the older lads told him to stop complaining or they'd throw him out of the car. So that put him in his place. We would normally start at eight o clock and sometimes we would make it in for the tea-break at ten o'clock.

You were driving up the Antrim Road, if you hadn't a full car, maybe you would have seen one of the lads out of work standing at a corner. If you'd have pulled into give him a lift, he ran off up the street – he thought it was a scoop. You'd usually have to run after and shout, "David, come on, it's us!" because at that time there was a lot of that went on; there was cars driving about and they would have attacked people – if they knew what side of the coin they were from, they would have attacked and so on. But everybody was tense and nervous about cars pulling in because at that time there were also lads being lifted off the streets by different cars just to be taken away, tortured and brutalised – you've heard about all that. There was always that sort of tenseness about it.

But once we got into work in the squad I worked in, there was a mixture of Protestants and Catholics and they got on the best, no bother to working nightshifts and helping one another. On another occasion, coming home from work, it was one particular period when there were a lot of vigilantes; usually young lads with a scarf tied round their face about 12-14 stopping you, playing soldiers they were, you know, in certain areas. We would have got one of the Protestant lads who would have come with us to get us through the roadblocks coming over towards the West Circular. When we got to the other side of West Circular we were okay at the Republican roadblocks. Similar situation with young lads with bats – they had a place to stop you and maybe a hundred yards further down, if you didn't stop, they were waiting with the stones and bricks to hammer your car with. I wouldn't say it happened very often, but it was something you were always aware of and conscious of and it created that tension.

The other amusing occasion I remember coming home from Michelin, we had finished at an eleven o clock shift and I had a full car that night but there had been two other lads left behind because their lift... somebody had phoned in and had to go on home and it was a terrible night; teeming out of the heavens, so we squeezed them in the back seat, so there was five in the back seat and two of us in the front. We had come down the Antrim Road and we were stopped by the UDR – the Ulster Defence Regiment, and I got out of the car to speak to the lad and he gave me the biggest dressing down about the numbers in the car. He then flicked up his visor which he was wearing – he says, "Alright, Stuartie, go on." He was a lad I worked with down at the oil refinery and he said, "If you see the police or the army stop you, don't tell them we stopped you"

Despite the inconvenience some people refused to co-operate with the security measures

I D

I also remember, that I used to give a lad a lift, and he refused to carry any identification.

That was his contribution to the struggle; that he wasn't going to cow down... which meant that when we were stopped, everyone was told to get out of the car as soon as he wouldn't identify himself... we all carried identification, but everybody was told to get out of the car and it was searched just to hold you up, because he wouldn't cooperate. No matter how often we appealed to him, he wasn't going to cow down to the forces of occupation.

In response to a sustained and ferocious bombing campaign by the Provisional IRA city and town centres across Northern Ireland were surrounded by 'a ring of steel', security fencing through which all pedestrians and vehicles entering were searched.

Security Checks

I remember the security check in town. The soldiers would tell you to open your coat. My friend and I were strong from drink and we refused. We were taken to the barracks on Royal Avenue and when we were released at 6 the next morning my husband was down waiting for me with his arms crossed. He was furious.

The impact of the bombing campaign on individual lives is reflected in this woman's memories.

Abercorn Bomb

I was working in the hospital when the Abercorn bomb went off. It was a Saturday afternoon. It was a terrible thing. They give us tweezers to sit and pull bits of wood out of people. There was this fella sat in a wheelchair and he said 'I'm alright, there's people worse than me'. When I went into work on the Monday and went and asked about him – the whole time I was sitting there he had a bit of wood in his chest. I think he was in shock or something. He had sat there all those hours in the wheelchair. When you think about all the people who lost their legs and their lives. There were two wee sisters; one was out shopping for her wedding. She lost her legs. I don't know if she got married because you only see her for that time. She was from the country somewhere.

The conflict disrupted life in many different ways. For Springfield Road Methodist Church it was to set the church on a path that eventually led to its closure in 2012.

Springfield Methodist

The Troubles made it very difficult for the church and for the congregation. A lot of people were put out of the Springfield Road area and moved to different places – the Girl's Brigade ended as the leader was one of those put out. The church and congregation became smaller because people didn't want to travel down through here. But the faithful ones would have come no matter what happened – they would have come if they could. Twice the church was set on fire. Then the big hall was burnt – it was really, really bad.

But the people who lived next door – Paddy and Mary – they were very good; they watched out for the church and it was them who phoned the fire brigade – they were very, very good. If we were stuck and we couldn't get through the gate, they would let us through their house.

We couldn't get back through into Woodvale Avenue with the gate being locked. So they said, knock our door – as long as we know who you are, we'll let you though. That was before the two houses started up as the Currach Community. The gate was open during the day and people got through but at night time – we would have came on a Monday night for the 'women's meeting' – and it was locked, we would have used Mary's and Paddy's house to get through. One night I was coming from the hospital and it was closed so I knocked Mary's door and my Grandson was with me – because his mum was in at the time – and she let us through which was good. The Catholic neighbours were very good. We can't complain about them.

Catholics and Protestants came together at the Church for the Wednesday group, even before Forthspring started. I went away with them to Corrymeela and I enjoyed some lovely times down there because it was then you got to know people and how friendly they were and there was a wee church in Corrymeela. You would go in there at night and they had a meeting for everybody and it was the first time that I had ever really done that and I found the people were really nice and friendly and you got to know them and you got to respect them. Now, saying that, the service wasn't about Catholic or Protestant – it was just singing and somebody speaking and things like that. Even my husband was there and he enjoyed the fellowship.

I remember it especially for that – bringing Protestants and Catholics together which I thought was good though some of the people didn't like it and some of the people left the church when Forthspring came along – a lot of people didn't like it. But we definitely couldn't afford to keep the church without getting those grants for Forthspring. Without them the church wouldn't have survived because we couldn't keep the heating on. Sometimes you just have to change. If you wanted the church to keep going – it was either that or really closing the church – so what did you have?

But it was much more than that. I liked the people. I think you have to get to know people. I think sometimes people are scared when they hear of – it's the same with ethnic groups – when you embrace people you're afraid of them taking over because a lot of people said then, "that's just the start of it – then you'll see the priests". Father Reynolds used to come. Now I know some people in the church wouldn't even shake hands with him on a Sunday morning. He came and I said, "that's a lot of trash; he's just an ordinary man" and they didn't shake hands with him which I didn't agree with. But I shook hands with him and I talked to him and I thought he was very nice; if something was on he would have joined in and done the dishes and all and I would have dried them and I got to know him and thought he was very nice. That doesn't mean to say I would change – you can still keep your own faith and belief and still get on with people but I do know that some people were scared of a priest taking over if the church did close. And it still hasn't happened.

For the staff of the Europa Hotel, 'Europe's most bombed hotel', the challenge was to stay open in the most difficult of circumstances. Their determination and commitment formed camaraderie and friendships.

Europa Hotel

I started in Europa in August '73. I think it was at the later part of '73, a couple of friends of mine said that Thin Lizzy were playing in the Romano's, upstairs in Upper Queen Street. So four of us went down to it. It was all mineral water and that type of thing. That was the first concert I ever went to, and it was in the centre of town and I was only allowed to go because it was the top end of town; just off Castle Street. At that time I had an older sister and she used to go down to the likes of the Starlight, which was down in Ann Street I think. That was for the more-or-less older ones; people who were 19-20. But that's the first concert I was ever at, the Thin Lizzy concert – in '73. I was 16. I think it was just the time 'Whiskey in the Jar' came out. That was out in '73.

But when the security gates came along or as they came along; that kind of made the City centre out of bounds for entertainment stuff. It was too dangerous for you to go into it. You know most of the town closed anyway at ten or eleven at night – there was nothing in the town for anybody.

When I worked in the Europa I was training to become a chef and I think while I look back at it, they were the best years of my life, despite the troubles and all those sorts of things. But you were meeting people of different religion. I socialised with Protestants in the Europa. That's the first time I really socialised with Protestants... because, you know, we were never brought up to be bigoted in any way; just treat them the way you meet them. That's the way my family were brought up. Even through the generations. So that was the first time I had actually met Protestants and actually socialised with them – have a drink with them and that kind of thing – get to know them. Working there was like one big happy family. At the same time too, you were trying to learn your trade – and it was hard work. But, through the times it was bombed you did your best to get into work, and no matter what, through the companionship with those with whom you worked, you just got through it. I loved working there.

I remember one time we were told to get out. There was a bomb scare – one of the bombs didn't go off. Somebody had driven with a bomb into the delivery bay one time and we were all told to get out, and the thing went off while we were standing outside it on the other side of the street; down near the Tech . But when I worked there I actually went through three or four of the bombings. It was just a part of... you know, you get used to it. It didn't faze you in any way. You know you were never scared to go to work; the only time you were afraid to go to work was maybe walking to work or something because of a drive-by shooting or something like that – because I remember going to work one morning and I walked down the Grosvenor. Whenever I got into work, I was told that there were two postmen shot dead on Northumberland Street on the Falls Road and that was the same time I was coming to work.

It was hard work, you were training and you did split-shifts. You'd start in the morning at 10 o' clock and maybe get the preparation ready for lunchtime, and after lunch, we got the preparation ready for that night. We took our break at half two/three clock then back again for half six for services, then start again at seven o' clock to half ten and you wouldn't get home to 12 o' clock at night.

In the afternoon we used to go to the pictures or something like that. You know, if three or four of us were working on split shifts, maybe we would have went to the ABC and watched a film...I remember going to watch The Sting in it; The Sting was out in, I think, '74.

I would usually get a taxi home if I was working late, more for safety than convenience. They usually provided us a taxi free. They understood that it was later on... it would have been risky. Maybe two people were going to the Falls and two people were going to the Shankill. One taxi took the lot – took the four of us. I remember I had a good lot of friends there.

The bombing brought people together. I think it made the people there stronger… that no matter how many times they bombed it, we were going to work on. In no time at all the hotel was back up and running again. Even through the Loyalist strike. It stayed open during that time. I remember one day we actually had to work by candles and make salads. We used to meet some of the famous people… Martin Bell – I remember meeting him a few times and I saw Ian Paisley and people like that.

This woman recalls the events surrounding her brother's stay in hospital after being shot.

'I'm Frankie Murphy'

There was the time my brother had been shot at the bottom of the Whiterock. He was shot with an SLR in the back and his whole stomach was blown out of him. It was like he had two belly buttons where the scars were. I was working at the Royal then. We decided that we had to get him out. The arrangement was I walked in with my uniform to visit him, but I walked straight down to the Gent's toilets – it was the old corridor in the Royal. I started talking to him because I got in before the visiting because I worked there. When the visitors all started they let them in together. He was in a wee side ward just when you come in. When the visitors came in, he walked out and walked down with all the visitors so that nobody would see him. The old Royal had the balcony outside the bottom of the ward. So he walked out the men's ward and up the lady's ward and out that way. One of the nurses in the lady's ward had seen him and shouted 'that prisoner's away'. How far he got was where the Queen's big statue was. My daddy had gone in and said, 'where is he?', and I said 'away to the toilet'. A soldier came in and looked under the bed and all. He said, 'where is he?' and I said, 'down to the toilet' and he said, 'I didn't know he could walk' – the soldier was sitting outside guarding him, you see. The next thing they come in and arrested me and my daddy and I had my youngest son with me – he was about 4. They took us all to the Springfield Road Barracks at St Paul's Chapel. They put my daddy in a room - my daddy knew nothing about it, you see – and me and my wee boy. My brother minded the children for me when I was working at night because my husband was doing shift work. They would say to my ones – soldiers are going to come look for you. They're going to come in here and say I want Thomas – what do you say? 'I'm Frankie Murphy' right, so they were used to changing their names. As we were sitting getting questioned, my Thomas says 'I want to go to the toilet'.

The soldier was at the door with a big rifle in hand and says 'I'll take him to the toilet' so he took his hand and just as the special branch says to me 'What's your son's name?' the soldier says to him 'What's your name?' And he said 'Frankie Murphy' and I said to the special branch 'Thomas'. They couldn't believe for all the size of him and he wasn't telling his proper name.

We got released because my brother hadn't been charged so he wasn't a prisoner. They couldn't do nothing on us because he could have walked out at any time. While this was going on for us they brought a judge down to the Royal and charged him, and brought him down to Musgrave Military Hospital. The funny thing was the special branch that was charging him got shot dead and he had the evidence and that and the charge was threw out of court.

Although security was a constant feature of life it was not necessarily as pervasive or as organized as it might have appeared.

Christmas Cake

When I was working I transferred down from the Royal to the Tech by the Black Man. I had gone back and got a few qualifications and got a job down in the School of Chiropractors. There was a girl there I knew from years ago – we worked together in a nurses home on Brunswick Street, she was a Protestant girl but I always kept in touch with her. I was talking to her about how I started baking Christmas cakes and she goes 'Ach, bake us one' and I says well 'alright'. At the time she was working at Queen Street Police Station as a cleaner. I said to her, I'll give you a shout when it's ready and you can come around and get it. Coming up the day before Christmas Eve I phoned her and said I have your Christmas cake here which I had in a biscuit tin and wrapped up in Christmas paper for her. When I stopped work there was no sign of her, so I went round to the police station with this tin and said, I want to go in and see her and they let me into the police station. I was sitting in the hall and they were calling her name over the intercom and there was no sign of her coming. One of the policewomen came and said, 'I think she went out to get messages, a few wee things she needs for Christmas. Can I help you?' And I said – I have a Christmas cake here for her and she says 'That's alright give it to me'. She took it off me, brought it in and set it on her desk. I walked out then and what hit me was there was so much security on and when I came into Castle Street and I just thought to myself – that could have been a bomb. Nobody checked it, nobody asked what's in it – I said it was a Christmas cake and they took my word for it. The policewoman took it and put it in the middle of the police station and set it on her desk and I just thought that could've been a bomb. Maybe they thought that I was a Protestant because I was looking her. When the girl phoned me that night to say she got the cake I told her I was really shocked the way I walked into the police station and they took that off me and they took my word that that was a Christmas cake. I said, 'That could have been a bomb'. She says 'I never thought of that, I never thought of that'. I'm sure when she went back to work after Christmas, I'm sure she said that to them. That was in the 70s.

This woman conveys the tragedy of her young cousin's killing and the unbearable sense of loss that resulted from it.

A bottle of sherry

My cousin worked at a garage and one of the pumps wasn't working. There was a car at one pump filling up and there was a car at the pump that was empty. She went out of the garage to tell the ones at the pump that's empty, you have to wait for the man – when they pulled out a gun and shot the fella that was filling his car. He never died, he got shot somewhere about the face. They drove away and the ambulance came and they had to give statements and all. She didn't get home until very late that night. She went into work the next day. About 12 o clock the people who done the shooting came back and shot her dead. The thing was one of the gunmen was known to her and he thought that she recognised him. They came back to silence her.

The thing about it was she used to wait on me and my husband going out, a Wednesday was our night out. I never had drink in the house but I won a bottle of sherry. I just happened this day to move stuff and the bottle of sherry was half empty. My own wee girl was 12 at the time and I said to her 'have you been drinking that?' 'No' so she told me that when we went out my cousins come in and have wee sips of that. And I thought, I'll say to her for drinking. The Wednesday night before she was shot we were going up the street and she was coming down with her chum. And I stood and let out a big yell. She knew by the way I shouted her name that she done something, and she run. When she died I was telling her mommy 'if she was alive now, you'd give her a bottle and say drink it'. It was a wee thing like that - I was going to shout at her for that but if she was alive you'd say 'here, take a drink'. I sat with her until she died, me and her daddy and her aunt. She just lay there until she had no blood left.

The Sunningdale Agreement, Northern Ireland's first power sharing agreement, was met with strong Unionist opposition. The Ulster Workers Council strike in May 1974 led to the collapse of the Executive, established under the terms of the Agreement in 1973.

Ulster Worker Council Strike

There was a sense of community. Everybody joined together. It was brilliant. It brought everybody out of their houses. The men were out and they had built a cooker with bricks and a grill. Somebody would have come out with a pot of tatties; somebody else with stuff to make stew and the whole street got it. And the men couldn't go to work. Or you would have seen some of the men putting their suits on by the way that they were going into the town, then changing into their boiler suits in Mackies to do their days work.

We got followed one night going into town. I used to clean in the town. It was our own ones following us. We were told not to come back out again the next night to work until everything was all over.

They brought the soldiers into man the electricity. You had to get your stuff all done at a certain time before the lights went off. The milk lorry came straight from the farm. You took your milk bottle down to St Matthews Church. It was exciting. You were getting ready to go to bed and you heard the bin lids going. My Dad ran to get his tin hat to go out. I remember sitting on a wee stool in the outside toilet and my mother on the toilet, a candle burning, listening to the peelers radio. 'Away and go and tell your da quick, there is a squad away up Disraeli Street'.

Working Through the Strike

I worked through the Ulster Workers Council strike because we needed the money. I'm just the type of person that nobody tells me what to do and my husband was the same – he went to work too. We both went to work and I think somebody said something but I wasn't worried about what they said. I was going to my work and a lot of people did – not just me. There was a lot of people who went to the Blackstaff at that time and they had to go through Blackmountain estate and they all came to work. But nobody ever did anything to the house because of us going to work.

People displayed differing levels of ingenuity during the conflict. Of necessity individuals and communities became more self-reliant. The spirit and resilience of people is often recalled with a mixture of pride and humour and an acceptance of lawlessness that may well appear inappropriate to many.

Petrol Bombs

We made the petrol bombs. We hide them in the house and outside in the manholes. This day I looked outside. There was heavy rain, the whole street was flooded. The petrol bombs were floating down Derry Street. I said let them go. My husband said, 'you couldn't let them go'. He sent me out to collect them and he stood at the door with a milk crate to put them back in again. Then someone squealed on us and they raided the house. They even searched the child's pram. All they got was tyres. They had the cheek to come back and buy the tyres. That was the police for you; they didn't do their job very well. They didn't find the petrol bombs, they were well away. We were wired off that they were coming.

Self-help took many forms. For these women it was about learning the skills to operate as a field hospital.

First Aiders

I hurt my leg. Down in the Clonard area there was lots of wood with the barricades. I was young, maybe eight. We took a plank of wood off the barricade to make a seesaw. Somebody shouted 'here's the Brits' and everybody dropped the plank of wood but I didn't. By the time I dropped the plank of wood it had lifted a lump out of my leg. I remember going down to my granny's to get the first aid done. I remember being slagged. They were taking the micky out of me. 'If you had of got the bit of skin we could have sewed it on'. 'Will we go back up and look for it'.

Things like that. In my granny's house the neighbours would be in and out all the time, she was very close to the women in the street. They were all first aiders. I remember being there one time when they were all there as a group, sitting in the wee parlour, all piled in, looking at these demonstrations of bandaging.

The threat of death and injury was both ever present and part of the everyday. It is recalled here almost as the norm, remembered not as a defining event in itself but as something located within the regular weekly schedule of baths and bed times.

Springfield Road Bomb

My brother was in the bath, the bathroom window came in on him in the bath. It would have been early enough in the evening. There wasn't a lot of hot water, I must have been in first because I was the girl and he was the boy. We were always put in our pyjamas about six o'clock at night and in bed for seven. As young children that was just the way my parents did it. It must have been early in the evening because the baths were going on. I remember someone coming to the door and their face was covered in blood. Then the army would have turned up. In those early stages, the army would have known first names; they were calling my Mummy by her first name. My impression was we went back and forth to my Mummy's mates all night long; they lived on the far side of the road from us. The street was evacuated and we all crowded into their house. Every time there was a bomb scare that is what we did. It seemed like it went on all night, but all night is a long time for a child.

As the city centre in Belfast became a virtual 'no go' zone in the evenings communities developed their own venues for entertainment.

Community Entertainment

There was no transport. Buses stopped at a certain time and you could not get out much. So round the areas people started having their own community entertainment like Clonard Hall. It was very good on a Tuesday night. Gerry Miller, remember? And we had a band and had great nights in it. Even at the beginning, when they were friendly with the army, they had them in at the concerts. You were afraid at night to go downtown. It was like a ghost town. There was nobody about. You would have gone into town to go to the pictures but then we went on weekend bus runs. We went to Bunratty Castle, the Rosses Hotel up in Donegal. And then at Christmas we had an annual bus run to Dublin. It was very good.

This story, and the one following, recalls very differing experiences of work during the Troubles.

Working Relations

We were in the electrical side and we were fairly well balanced in numbers because there were five sparks and two helpers in each shift and it was just a fair mixture each time. We went out socialising on occasions; we'd arranged a bit of a do if somebody was leaving or some event, we went up to one of the pubs close at hand and had a drink together.

I was lucky; I had damaged my finger, so I was off on the sick during most of the Ulster Worker's Council strike. I was off for about six weeks or so, so I was very lucky in a way.

I found that people just wanted to get to work and get on with their work and I'm quite sure there were some of them there that would have been active outside their working hours... but in work there was never any hostility or any bother. We had that relationship at least among the squads where I worked in – I never had any worries or fears from those people about going to work. In fact, coming out on many a winter's morning up on Mallusk or the hills, if your car wouldn't start, everybody pitched into help everyone else to get their cars going.

The biggest problem was getting to work and sometimes getting home. Sometimes if you were finishing at eleven, the lads would come in and say, 'Lads, you needn't try to get through Belfast tonight; it's completely blocked with roadblocks'. There was a back road over the hills by a place near Dundrod. You had to drive on down there and go drop the lads off at the bottom of the Springfield Road, so it could be 1 o clock in the morning before you got home at night.

Signs and Symbols

The section that actually calculated the wages on a weekly basis was right beside where I sat and they had 'page 3' images all over the walls and there were young women working in the department too and I objected to this and felt that it was dreadful – anybody visiting personnel had to walk past this and what impression was it creating? That didn't change immediately and I was called all kinds of things, like I was a "prude" or "frigid" or whatever they felt was wrong with me – they supposed I would close down all the art museums. It did change, a few years later.

But there were rules about signs and symbols. You weren't allowed to display sectarian signs and symbols in the office place which I thought was very good. So, you couldn't have flags being displayed.

In those days it was very much about fairness and neutrality, that if people came to us in genuine distress, they would be dealt with by a set of policies that applied to everybody – you know, that there were proper procedures that hadn't been there when it had been the councils that had been in charge of housing. The other thing is, don't forget, housing was the hot issue that led to people taking to the streets in the first place because it was so outrageously unfair what was happening.

There was an awareness of that. When we would do inductions with new staff that would be one of the things we would say. You know, we were very proud that we had a selection scheme that people from the rest of the UK would come to us to talk and find out about because they hadn't got it as well thought out as us - how you awarded houses when there was always a greater demand than there was a supply. And people would come and visit the Housing Executive from all over Europe because they were impressed with how we were dealing with accommodating difference.

CHAPTER 3
1980s

Backdrop – Hunger Strikes- Carolyn - Walking to Work– Working in the Royal – Travelling Home – The Big Smoke – A Foot in both Camps – A Big Inconvenience – Bomb Scares – Searching – The Unions.

Backdrop: Walls come tumbling down

The 1980's began with a deep seated economic recession. The fiscal response of increasingly right wing governments was deregulation and lower taxes that gave rise to greater inequality and would eventually lead to the banking crisis of 2008. The period of economic hardship fuelled social division and conflict. Margaret Thatcher and Ronald Reagan became firm friends as unemployment topped three million in the UK and nuclear missiles arrived at Greenham Common. Britain and Argentina fought the Falklands War. Solidarity formed in the Gdańsk shipyard in Poland. In China protest reached the world stage with the Tiananmen Square massacre. The Chernobyl disaster represented the worst nuclear disaster to date as the Soviet nuclear power suffered the meltdown of its reactor with the explosion resulting in a radioactive cloud across Europe. The Cold War ended in the symbolic moment of the beginning of the dismantling of the Berlin Wall (also known as the 'Anti-Fascist Protection Rampart') in November 1989.

Michael Jackson was the most successful artist of the decade. Prince and Madonna were the cool superstars and ecstasy fuelled acid house dance music and raves. John Lennon was shot and killed outside his New York home in December 1980. Television went truly global with the number of television sets worldwide almost doubling with dramatic increases in ownership in China and India. The internet made its first faltering steps towards creating a whole new virtual world. By the end of the decade almost 1 million Americans were users. Meanwhile the Rubik's cube kept young and old uselessly occupied.

In the North of Ireland divisions deepened. The 1980's was the darkest of decades in Northern Ireland. Although statistically the number of deaths was lower than the previous decade, the battle lines were well established and the conflict bitter. The decade began with the Hunger Strikes. The second hunger strike, in 1981, led to the death of 10 Provisional IRA prisoners. The funeral of the hunger strike leader, Bobby Sands, who had been elected as MP for Fermanagh South Tyrone, was attended by an estimated 100,000 people. The hunger strikes lasted for seven months and were one of the most violent periods of the conflict with 61 deaths. In 1984 the IRA, in an attempt to kill Thatcher and the British cabinet, bombed the Grand Hotel in Brighton.

The Anglo- Irish Agreement in 1985 gave the Irish government an advisory role in Northern Irish matters, whilst confirming that the constitutional position of the state would not change without majority consent. Unionist opposition took the form of a mass rally at Belfast City Hall and a subsequent Day of Action in 1986. All unionist MP's resigned their Westminster seats, forcing by-elections.

As the decade came to an end violence continued. In 1988 the killing of 3 unarmed IRA members in Gibraltar by the SAS was quickly followed by Michael Stone's attack at Milltown Cemetery and the subsequent killing of the two Corporals. Death followed death in an apparent unending cycle of brutality. Yet this period is credited with containing within it the seeds of the Peace Process as people in all sections of society felt it was time to crawl back from the abyss. The secret Hume/Adams talks were underway. Father Alec Reid from Clonard Monastery played a central role in facilitating the talks with Gerry Adams describing Clonard 'as the cradle of the peace process'.

On the Springfield Road Lanark Way was built to link the Shankill to the Springvale industrial park. The new route was controversial as it provided an escape route for sectarian killers and the gate placed towards the Springfield Road end became a site for violence and unrest. By this stage the road was defined by the violence of the past decade and in the recollections of many local people is likened to a warzone, bleak, desolate and carrying the scars of violence.

The decade began with the Hunger Strikes and, arguably, the most polarized set of relationships between people in the North of Ireland during the whole period of the conflict.

Hunger Strikes

It was nearly like excitement, I'm ashamed to say. I was sixteen at the time. It was the in thing to do. Bobby Sands was the first to die. Everybody came out over the hunger strikers. Everybody came out, nobody stayed in their house.

We were walking round, my aunt and all. Because I was sixteen I couldn't get a proper cap for my tooth, I had a temporary one. It was a wee bit of a tooth and a matchstick went up into the gum. On the way round we were talking that much and carrying on, the cap flew out. We all got down looking for the tooth, it was right in the front, you couldn't be seen without it, you would be scundered. I had to spend the rest of the time holding it in. My aunt gave me a bit of chewing gum to stick it in. We all went round and queued up to see the body. I can still see his face in the coffin. There was an armed guard at the top and the bottom of the coffin, masked of course. I can see his face in the coffin, the gauntness of it, the sunken cheeks; it really was like a skeleton with skin on it. That night or that weekend there was a lot of rioting. There were burnt out cars on our road. A plastic bullet came through a window in our house and landed in my baby brother's cot. The funeral came up. I never saw so many people in my life. The service was broadcast on loud speakers. It was serious. Walking round to see the coffin, the journey round was a bit of a carryon but once you seen the coffin it did impact on you. You began to question things more, wanted to know what was happening. My young brother was arrested; the army said he was in a photograph taken during rioting. He was interrogated but then released. It was a case of mistaken identity.

During 1981, the year of protests and rioting surrounding the hunger strikes, the security forces fired over 29,000 plastic bullets, causing seven deaths and numerous injuries to adults and children.

Carolyn

I was a little older than Carolyn. I think she was eleven when she was murdered. It seemed to impact more seriously on me than the hunger strikers did; don't know why, maybe because she was young. We all went to see her in the coffin. I remember the house was empty. The furniture had been taken out because crowds came to visit her. At that time there was a lot of kids getting hit with plastic bullets.

You had Julie Livingstone. Every time you turned on the TV there was another child getting hit by a plastic bullet. You didn't always take what was going on seriously. My opinion and my parent's opinion would have been different. They could see the seriousness of it all. It hit me hard because she was a child, it could have been me and because I knew her. She was only going across the street to get milk or something. You were saying to yourself 'I walk across that street every day to do the exact same thing'. It could have been me.

It was the first funeral for me. I had been to see people in a coffin before but it was the first time I had seen anything like that before. There were crowds, you were nearly queuing up, it was like queuing up for a fairground ride.

I remember my mummy bringing stuff to the house although my mummy wouldn't have necessarily knew them.

The deaths at the start of the eighties spread fear and uncertainty throughout the community.

Walking to Work

I remember walking up one winter morning – dark – walking up the Springfield Road and there was a car parked outside the Methodist church, or near the Methodist church, and I had to walk between this car and the wall obviously and I thought to myself, "Gosh" and for a second or two I felt apprehensive. I thought to myself, "I could get shot here" and I suppose if I had turned and ran I could still have got shot but by that time there was no way out. So I walked on into Mackie's; it was okay.

Working in the Royal

We used to come up the road in a gang, you would say, when I worked in the Royal. It felt safer. One night I said, "Can I get home early? I need to get home." And the boss said, "Certainly. You go." She let me go and a bomb went off at Springfield Road Barracks. It went off just as I had got to my own house. The next night I went in she said, "Do you know something?" and I said, "What?" and she replied, "My heart was in my mouth last night." I asked why and she replied, "If I had been caught on letting you leave early" to which I replied, "never mind that I could have been blown to bits!" We laughed that night about that. But that was the sort of thing you did laugh about. That was the risk you took – if I had have waited ten or fifteen minutes I could have been caught up in that. I've had lucky escapes. I think that applies to everybody. People come and say to you "Wait 'till you hear what happened to me; I was nearly shot" or, "I was nearly blew up" or, "I was hurt." But you don't have that fear now; that fear's gone. We all worked in different parts of the Royal but they used to open the gate at 9:00 and let us all out. We used to meet up and stand at 8:55 and then anyone who worked round here – we all walked up together. I was always the last to leave because the rest all live further down. I used to walk up cut through one of the streets and come up the back. I never ever walked the front of the Springfield Road. We all walked up. Honestly, it was like pensioner's convention; all hobbling up the road. And then a girl who worked in the Royal moved up beside me, which was better for me because then I had company the whole way up. Many a night she and I ran that road. If we had have heard a noise it was like fire coming out of our heels. But thank God it's all away now. It's all gone.

Travelling Home

Sandra worked in the hospital and when the gates went up at the bottom of Workman's Avenue – they were closed, I think at suppertime. She was talking to me one day and saying that to get home she had to go all the way into town because the gates were closed. So she had to get the bus down into town and then a bus up the Shankill Road. So it put an hour on her working day really. Whereas if she'd been able to go through the gate, you know, ten minutes it would have taken to walk up the road here. And I happened to say to her that I knew Paddy and May who lived in the house beside Forthspring and I took her round one night and introduced her to them. Their house was both sides of the peace line, so they had an entrance that took you out into

Workman Avenue, so they said to Sandra, "Certainly, no problem", so she used to walk up, if the gate was locked, rapped Paddy and May's door and they took her through the house, and through the back door and out into Workman Avenue. It's a bit like Forthspring itself; you know the front of it is on one side of the peace line and the back of it on the other. It literally straddles the peace line.

This young man, a child in the mid-eighties, recalls the violence and the sense of chaos surrounding his upbringing.

It was crazy then.

We lived at New Barnsley. We had a police station right at the bottom – Henry Taggar that was our local police station. There was always the coming and going every hour. And there were such riots and kerfuffle outside it. I haven't got a recollection of the early days, though my grandmother does, when they had the bin lids and stuff. She told me the story of the bin lids and the protesting and different things. When you were growing up you seen plastic bullets being fired; a friend of mine was at the top of a lamp post and got shot in the head. He's still alive to tell the tale. He was on a lamp post. He was up... I don't know what he was doing, but he was up the lamp post and he got shot by a plastic bullet. This guy is about three or four years older than me – so he would have been about eleven or twelve at the time. It was just stuff like that when you actually just seen this. It was crazy then. Now that you're grown up, you ask yourself of the young people now – if they seen that, how would it affect them? It's just good that it's over.

The bitterness and the fear drove people away.

The Big Smoke

Kilkelly, Ireland, 18 and 60, my dear and loving son John
Your good friend the schoolmaster Pat McNamara's so good
As to write these words down.
Your brothers have all gone to find work in England
Kilkelly, Peter Jones

I was young, 18, but I had already lost a lot of very close friends – and all young lads. One was killed by the army, one was killed in a sectarian attack, one was killed in the streets by being out and involved or maybe not involved in the rioting – those things happened. I wasn't feeling I was able to cope with this. And there was an urge to see the world that would have prompted me to go anyway, like a lot of young people. So the two things together made it a sort of no-brainer. We went to Camden Town and we were told about a priest who would help you out. I can't even remember his name. For a day or two we were sleeping in a park. The priest got us a job and he also got us accommodation – they went together. I was working in a pub. One of my big memories of that time was the landlord saying, "Look, you know, we've got you a job, we've got you accommodation – you're going to have to get your hair cut." I was devastated by this. I had hair down to my waist and after that, every time I walk past that barber – and it's still there – just beside Hammersmith Tube station, I think of that and I remember the guy made fun of me; he called me a girl and said, "You shouldn't be in here; you should be going to the girls." My two friends went back after about a month. I said I was going to give it another six months if it didn't work out. I never actually went back to Belfast after that to live. I found my place in England. This idea of neither here nor there, I felt very much there. And in some ways I maybe lost a bit of here in the process. You know, I did experience racism, particularly during times of tension, like bombing campaigns. I always think that English people, particularly Londoners, in general, are very tolerant people. I know it doesn't look like that sometimes, but to me that was my experience. And also to others as well; not just me, but to other people who came in. I will say I did feel like an immigrant. Being away from your family is not easy and I don't know if you've ever heard of a song that was based on letters found in an attic in America. They were letters from someone's relatives, letters from home. The letters set out all the things that happened at home that you would expect, like the births, weddings, and fall-outs – all of that – and he's reading it through letters. Always the letters ended, you know: when are you coming back? It's been a long time, we want to see you, but he never did go back. In some ways I felt a wee bit, not as extreme as that, but I felt a wee bit like that. So you did feel a bit out of it. When my father took ill I wasn't there to help him, like the rest of them did. But my brother said to me, "look, you know, your Da was an immigrant, you're an immigrant and your Da would have done exactly the same as you." Because that's what he did do in a sense – life was here and that was it, you don't beat yourself up about it – that's the way it is.

Throughout the decade segregation and division continued to increase as communities sought to find ways to protect themselves and in the search for safety barricaded the areas and drew in upon themselves.

Barriers

You know, it was a quiet, mixed area – not hard line in anyway. But that summer it became hard line. And suddenly we were on the nationalist side of this fence.

We'd just been on a lovely holiday to France. We had a really old Peugeot 504; I learned how to say cylinder head gasket in French which is not what everybody wants to learn on holiday ....so it was a holiday that was kind of tinged with some stress. And then the fan belt went on the way back which nearly ended with us missing our ferry across to Larne. But anyway, we were driving home at about 4 o' clock in the morning – "Great! We're nearly home" – and we get into the street and the church is normally in front of us – and it's demolished. We're thinking; "Do you think our house is still there?" do you know? The house was there but there was a big wall – well not a wall, it was fencing. Quite high fencing had been erected to separate the street and the new houses that had just been handed over were burnt, people had moved in but they'd been put out because I think there'd been an attempt to kind of mix – do a bit of shared housing and it hadn't worked. The barrier is still there. You had a family called the Murphy's who refused to move. It had been a terraced street and they refused to move, so the redeveloped houses; they all went. They were lovely new houses and they were demolished on that summer of '87 and what remained was the Murphy's – now detached and the barrier wove 'round it. And there they were.

In an environment of fear and mistrust, where loyalty to your own community was demanded and expected, being an outsider was not easy.

A Foot in Both Camps

I came from the Shankill and was married and living in the Falls, and the Troubles put me in an awful awkward position. It was very good before the

Troubles; everything was going quite well but when we got into these Troubles I realised it was an awkward because, as I say, I had a foot in both camps. But it became that I had a place in neither because the troubles brought about this idea you had to be identified with one side or the other, otherwise you were a traitor to your own kind. So that left me in a sort of a limbo. Although, to be quite honest I didn't sense it at the time it was just occasions when you would have a group of people and have joined a company, you sensed that their conversation changed because you were not one of them – you hadn't had a loyalist/protestant soccer background or Gaelic hurling background. This is another thing I remember – I remember one time whenever I was talking about playing for the Boy's Brigade, lads would stand around saying, "there's a lad from Andersonstown playing for the Boy's Brigade – how does that come about?" So that's when I learned just to watch what I said in company. The lads would appreciate it if you're working with them, helping one another out. They didn't care who you were or what you were but there were situations when you had to be very careful who you were going to be identified with and that made it a bit awkward. You didn't want to put the spotlight on them. And with your own family, well they could have had some criticism if one of their family was seen as having let the side down.

Whilst the violence and the bitterness persisted, a sense of exhaustion, of tiredness and frustration with it all grew.

A Big Inconvenience

It's funny how it changes. By the time I was 18 or 19 it was a nuisance. You were fed up with it. I worked in a supermarket. You were always getting put

out for bomb scares. We were all in the warehouse and you used to look around and say 'why can't we all go outside with customers in the car park. If a bomb goes off we are dead.' You know what I really hated? We had to put all their shopping back on the shelves, big trolley loads full of the week's shopping. The customers got fed up and went home. I remember one time there was death threat came through that any Catholics who worked in the place was going to be shot. Now the manager, funnily enough, was a Catholic despite where the supermarket was based. He ignored the threat so we all had to ignore it. The novelty of the Troubles wore off. You had battled down to the city centre to do your Christmas shopping; you had been searched that many times, your bags and belongings, going in and out of shops. You had maybe spent ages picking something and you were queuing up to pay for it, then there is a bomb scare announced and everybody is out. You had just wasted your entire night. By the time I had got to eighteen or nineteen it was a big inconvenience for me.

But for others the Troubles were simply a way of life.

Bomb Scares

I worked in Dorothy Perkins in Castle Court. All the shops would have put a yellow card up to let the staff know there was the possibility of an incendiary device in the shop. You would have had to go through the clothes to check there were no devices. They would have put the devices in the pocket of a coat or trousers. They used the card rather than alarm the customers. Sniffer dogs used to walk around Castle Court. I worked as well in City Cabs. It was mixed, ours went everywhere. There was always bomb scares on the Friday. All round the town. That was just normal. You just had to explainto people when they phoned for a taxi what was going on. You were used to all that then.

Searching

You got stopped at the gates going into the town and on the buses. My aunt came home from England for a holiday. I took her down to Castle Court. We were driving down round the back. I think it was the day after it opened. I was driving and I seen this fella I used to work with. I thought what is he doing

here. He says 'Can you open your boot and your bonnet?' I says 'what are you doing here, Jimmy?' He says 'Security'. Jimmy was a bit of a slice less than a loaf. So I say to him 'Do you know what a bomb looks like? Here he was 'No, I'm just looking'. I opened my bonnet and my boot and then he shouts over 'Bomb!' My aunt turned colours, I turned colours. And all these guns turned round and the police came over. Here he was to the policeman, 'I'm only codding'. He was sacked soon after that.

The following week I took the Aunt down again. There was a bomb scare. They wouldn't let me get my car out. I had to send her home in a taxi. I had to wait four hours to get back into my car. It was a nightmare.

Throughout the conflict attempts were made to encourage an end to violence. The trade union movement promoted a number of initiatives including the 'Better Life for All' campaign and at various stages of the conflict, particularly at moments of heightened tension or in response to specific atrocities, mass rallies were staged.

The Unions

I think the union did have some restraining role, but I didn't think they had a big enough active role in calming situations and encouraging harmony. I think it came from the men themselves, who realised they had to get to work and had to earn a living. I can't remember influence, officially, from the unions.

The unions might have done more but it was difficult. A lot of the unions were unbalanced in the membership. So, they had to be very careful too, they had to walk within the lines. Where we were working there was a fairly balanced workforce, which was unusual. I remember one occasion when we were called out by a Loyalist grouping who had called for a bit of a strike and a lot of our lads went out on strike and they were bantering. We thought if we weren't going to go out before when we were called by other sides, we weren't going to go out because it was the UDA, we weren't going to support that. Some of them went down the street, but there was never any ill will or feeling; it was a bantering match, "Hey you eejits, what are you going out there for", you know.

CHAPTER 4
1990s

Backdrop –John Judge- Shankill Bomb - Rioting - Ceasefires– The Wrong Shop – Springfield Road Rioting – Rioting – Ceasefire and Peace

Backdrop: Ceasefires and Agreement

Internationally the 90's was a decade of relative peace and prosperity. The end of the Cold War and the collapse of the Soviet Union created a period of calm for economic expansion and growth. No one was more confident than Francis Fukuyama, who asserted in his 1989 essay 'The End of History' that Western liberal democracy represented the pinnacle of human achievement. However, the peace was marred by violent and vicious ethnic conflicts in Africa and the Balkans with genocide in Rwanda and Bosnia. Peace in Northern Ireland became a global story. At the start of the decade Nelson Mandela was released from prison beginning the process that resulted in the end of apartheid in South Africa. Germany was reunited. The Irish Republic in the second half of the decade went through the remarkable period of economic growth referred to as the 'Celtic Tiger'.

Musically grunge and gansta rap emerged from America with Nirvana and Kurt Cobain the leading figure. In Britain the derivative Brit Pop formed part of the wider Cool Britannia culture and, in a sign of the times, the Spice Girls became the most successful British group since the Beatles and the Rolling Stones. In the most significant event of the decade the internet began to shape culture and commerce with an annual growth of 100%, year on year, of internet traffic from the mid '90s onwards.

The '90s were a time of change in Northern Ireland. This was not initially apparent. The Shankill bomb in October 1993 killed ten people, nine civilians and one of the two Provisional IRA bombers. Fourteen people were killed in the week following the bomb, eight of them in an attack on the Rising Sun Bar in Greysteel by the UDA. The long running conflict showed signs of ending with the IRA ceasefire in August 1994, soon followed by the loyalist ceasefire in October of the same year. This was a time of celebration and optimism. The US President, Bill Clinton, came to Belfast, shook hands off camera with Gerry Adams and switched on the Christmas tree lights. Although the IRA ceasefire collapsed in 1996 it was re-instated in 1997. Peace talks resulted in the Belfast/Good Friday Agreement in 1998 with copies distributed to all households in Northern Ireland. The mood was upbeat as majorities in the North and South of Ireland voted in favour of the Agreement in May 1998. David Trimble, leader of the Ulster Unionists and John Hume, SDLP leader, were jointly awarded the Nobel Peace Prize 'for their efforts to find a peaceful solution to the conflict in Northern Ireland'. However, the Agreement was more enthusiastically embraced by Nationalists than Unionists and faced opposition from Ian Paisley's DUP and James Molyneaux, former leader of the Ulster Unionist Party. Unionist anger found a focus in parading disputes, including Drumcree and opposition to the Parades Commission, established in 1998. In August of the same year 29 people died as a result of the Omagh Bomb, planted by dissident republicans opposed to the Good Friday Agreement.

During his visit to Belfast in 1995 Bill Clinton visited the Mackies factory on the Springfield Road and spoke of how Northern Ireland had 'a chance not only to begin anew, but to be a real inspiration to the rest of the world, a model of progress through tolerance'. Mackies closed in 1999. The promised new Springvale campus of the University of Ulster never materialized. Forthspring opened in 1997, growing out of a partnership between Springfield Methodist Church, Cornerstone Community, Currach Community and Mid Spring Community Association.

A decade once again began with death and sorrow.

John Judge

We were only nine months in the street when one of our neighbours was murdered. He was actually in the garden when the fellow was shot dead. So the people decided to get out and block Lanark way because they said they took that route to escape and there was rioting down there and the other side was coming out because the Catholics were in Lanark way with placards and whatever. One fellow actually got knocked down; a car sped up and hit him, so that started a full-scale riot. It was bad what happened to the fellow in our street. John was at his own kid's birthday party, standing out front.

My wee boy had been at the birthday party – he was twelve, he and his friend. It was a terrible night because we didn't have the railings on the top of our walls at the time and my wall just went straight round and my husband was sitting on the wall with his back out towards the Springfield Road and there was a mini-series on and I called him in and I said, "I'm going to make a cup of tea so if you want to watch this mini-series come on in." It was a beautiful night and both doors were lying open and he lay down on the settee to watch this mini-series and the next thing we heard was the shooting. We ran up the street and my wee girl who was about 14 at the time, she said, "daddy, there's somebody lying here." He had worked in a hospital and he had done a first aid course and approached the man to check how badly injured he was but he said, "No, he's dead. He's definitely dead." They shot him in the back of the head.

The whole street was involved and it was terrible at that time too – for that girl and her three kids too. A lot of people moved out. If you had have seen the people who moved out of that street following that; there were about eight families that moved out. But we said, why should we move out? We had got good houses; we had lived in dumps for years and we had got good houses and we said, "No, we're not going to move."

Everybody was watching everybody and no matter what stranger came into the street, you were in with your door locked, looking out to see who they were looking for; you were afraid to open the door. The housing executive actually put in peepholes so you could see anybody who came to your door.

In the following story the normal pattern of division and separation promoting further division is over-turned as a barrier brings two women together in a common cause.

Unexpected Consequences

My daughter-in-law was involved in establishing MISCA, the Mid Spring Community Association. She lived in a flat opposite the police station on Springfield Parade. The area was mixed, though mainly Protestant. This was 1991. Her son played in the street, often with another boy, a neighbour's son. The two mothers rarely spoke, perhaps only when there were disagreements between their sons. A barrier was erected at the end of West Circular Road, blocking traffic from accessing the Springfield Road. All the traffic, including buses, was diverted along Springfield Parade and this quickly became a nightmare, particularly with the children used to playing in the street. Marie, along with another woman, started a petition to stop the buses using the street. As they got signatures and talked to people they began to realize that people wanted a community association and they decided to do something about it.

The Shankill bomb exploded on Saturday, 23rd October 1993, killing ten people including one of the bombers.

Shankill Bomb

All I remember is running up the road looking for my daughters. I was round in the house. They had gone out shopping that morning and I heard the noise. I went round the corner, people were hysterical. People were running everywhere and the dust. I found them and took them in my arms. I was so glad to see them. I feel bad about it sometimes but in that sort of situation you are bound to think of your own first. The next days were terrible. All the funerals and I kept thinking that could have been my daughters. I still think that.

Following the Hume/Adams talks, the Downing Street Declaration by the British and Irish governments in 1991, the involvement of the Irish Taoiseach, Albert Reynolds and a number of high profile gestures including the granting of a US visa to Gerry Adams, the IRA declared a ceasefire in 1994.

Ceasefires

The first ceasefire I didn't really believe. Most people didn't believe it – we kept waiting on it breaking and breaking and breaking and then it dragged on and on the news, "yes they're going to do it, no they're not going to do it." The second ceasefire was great – happy days, you know, your children aren't going to go through this anymore. I had a big gap between my youngest and my oldest and I was thinking, "Ah, my youngest isn't going to have to see none of this... it's all going to go" well violence I mean, I'm not saying I wasn't naive enough to think that everything was going to go back to the way it was immediately, but the end of violence and the fear. That turned out to be, in my life, right, because my youngest son just goes anywhere now and I don't really have any worries about him going into different places or different parts of the city. I'm happy enough with him to do that, whereas with the oldest if he had said he was going to different parts of the city, I'd have a heart attack.

The IRA ceasefire was followed by a statement by the Combined Loyalist Military Command(CLMC) on 13th October 1994, also declaring a ceasefire. The new found peace in Northern Ireland brought the US president to Northern Ireland in November 1995.

The Wrong Shop

Bill Clinton, when he came to the Shankill, was supposed to come up to where the bomb had been on the Shankill, which was Stevenson's fruit shop. But he didn't. He stopped at Violets. It was his security; they took him to the wrong fruit shop. The traffic was terrible. The security was unreal as if the town had just stopped. They were all talking up their sleeves, the security men. Nothing happened if they didn't say it happened.

Despite the peace process at a local level violence persisted, often prompted by disputes over parading.

Springfield Road Rioting

We had a baby in the house, yes. One night he was in a baby walker and he fell down steps and he cut his head. We picked him up to bring him to the hospital and we were coming out on to the front of the road when somebody threw a brick so we turned to go down the back way and the army were coming up and they said, "is there anything wrong?" I told them that there was a wee bit of rioting up there and told them that someone just threw a brick at us. I said, "That child has already cut his head as he fell, we're taking him to the hospital." So they came up and said, "It's alright. You go on and we'll go up and sort this out." So they told us just to go on down the back and get him checked out. That was very scary too because we didn't know how badly hurt he was. There were mainly fellas involved in the rioting but there were girls too. The rioting between Protestants and the Catholics was nearly every night. One night there was one really bad riot and I mean it was terrible. Everyone was shouting and panicking and squealing. I think there were a couple of houses wrecked that night. It was awful. It was nearly like being in the heart of the Troubles again, because everybody was out in their pyjamas and slippers screaming and shouting, "Get the police, get the army, and get the papers." I don't think anybody slept the rest of that night. To be honest with you that peace wall was a godsend at the time, because it kept the sides apart and you got a night's sleep.

Rioting

On this side, there was a derelict garage at which they were all rioting one night and we were getting out to make sure none of ours... to get them all in. There was an old man who lived on his own at the other side of the road and there was this single girl who went up to make sure he was alright – I think you called him Paddy, he was a piano teacher. Paddy was alright but she got smashed up the head with a brick. So she was lying at the corner – it was so funny and it wasn't funny – she was lying at the corner and the blood was pouring out of her head so her friend decided that she would go up to see if she was alright. So she got up and she got hit and she was lying at the corner. So there were casualties on this side of the road. Then an ambulance flies up the road, collects the injured from this side of the road, puts them in the ambulance, goes over to the other side of the road, puts the injured from that side of the road into the ambulance so all the rioters go in the ambulance together. We were kicking ourselves, we were saying that that ambulance will be rocking and rolling down that road. They were beating the hell out of each other and the next thing there were all put into an ambulance and taken to the hospital. Through it all there were funny times but most of the time you were scared out of your wits – you really were scared. Alright, people got injured during rioting but rioting wasn't as serious as shooting. It was the shooting you had to watch; once you heard the shooting that was it, everybody came indoors and locked themselves in.

Ceasefire and Peace

It was the 31st August 1994. I was on a plane to Cyprus. I think the pilot gave out the news of the IRA ceasefire. It was a package tour; all the passengers were from Belfast. I remember my reaction, I was pleased.

I was down South in the summer of 1996. I was getting married and we were saving up so we didn't have much money for a holiday. We were camping during the Twelfth week and we were totally oblivious to Drumcree. We arrived back home to the news of all the trouble. We had been talking about marriage and children and decided not to have children in the North. We talked of leaving the country. Looking back now we both regret we didn't pay more attention to what we were saying. We married and in 1997 something changed and we decided it was ok to have children here. We also talked about where we would live and thought of living in a Protestant area and then we thought of how it might be for the children walking home and decided to live in a Nationalist area. My husband had memories of being picked on as a child as a Catholic. We stayed and had children because of the Good Friday Agreement. In the late nineties things could not have been better. The children came along; we were living in our new house, in our own world. I must have been in a wee bubble. If the kids move country to work, whether its America, Australia or Canada, we will get up and move abroad as well. It doesn't feel now like much has changed. Nothing has changed.

CHAPTER 4
2000s and onwards

Backdrop – Dalai Lama – Whiterock Parade –How did we cope? – Forthspring – Since the Good Friday Agreement – The Troubles shaped my life - We're a bit happier.

2000 began, as predicted by Nostradamus, with the new Millennium and fireworks in Sydney harbour. Despite the prophets of doom the world did not end, nor did computers crash. There was no millennium bug. The internet grew rapidly and globalization gathered pace. The economic and political dominance of the United States, fuelled by the end of the Cold War and economic growth, went into reverse. The September 11 attacks vividly represented the conflict between Western capitalist states and Al Qaeda and gave rise to what became known as the War on Terror and the invasion of Afghanistan. The decade closed with economic recession following the global financial crisis.

Musically, product was remarketed and re-issued, as music went on line with i-Tunes. Bands went on mega-tours as record sales declined and Robbie Williams, Eminem and Beyoncé were the bestselling artists. Harry Potter raised literature to new heights and fantasy swamped Hollywood with the ubiquitous Harry Potter, Lord of the Rings and Avatar.

The decade began as it was to continue in Northern Ireland with political fallout and disagreement. The Assembly was suspended from October 2002 to May 2007. Decommissioning by paramilitary organizations began in 2001 and became a long drawn out political squabble, delaying progress. The Holy Cross dispute, in which loyalist protestors blocked Catholic children going to school, damaged community relations and reminded everyone, if it was necessary, that sectarianism and division remained a continuing feature of life in the North of Ireland. The St. Andrews Agreement between the British and Irish governments and the political parties in Northern Ireland, based on multi-party talks in 2006, led to the creation of a new Executive in 2007 and the election of Ian Paisley and Martin McGuinness as First and Deputy First Minister.

The Industrial Development Board purchased the vacant Mackies site and created the Springvale Business Park in 2001. It remains unoccupied. Rioting and violence were an ever present possibility with major rioting following the

postponed Whiterock Parade in 2005. In more recent years a degree of accommodation has resulted in a managed and peaceful marching season. Springfield Primary School celebrated its centenary in 2010. In 2012 the Belfast Metropolitan College opened a learning centre, the E3, building on part of the land earmarked for the intended Springvale Campus.

Today, 2014, it's fair to say that the older you are, the better you tend to feel about the Peace Process. Older people remember the dark days when death and violence were a daily occurrence. However, widespread disillusionment exists with the political process, parading and the flags protest illustrate continuing divisions as does the continuing struggle over the past itself. The need for understanding, dialogue and reconciliation remains as strong as ever.

As Northern Ireland was feted worldwide as a good news story some exotic visitors washed up on our shores and even found their way to the Springfield Road.

Dalai Lama

When Bill Clinton came to Mackie's in 1995 he passed by in the car along the road. The only one who walked along there was the Dalai Lama; he was the only one who walked through the Workman Avenue gates, with Tibetan prayer flags hanging on the gates. I thought it was great. He came down

Workman and I think he came along Kirk or Workman and a bit of Kirk. Anyway, he stopped just where the two of those meet and that would be roughly the front of our house and that was great.

It was lovely; just realising that these gates open for nobody, only the Orangemen, but they opened for somebody of a different faith and both sides were trying to celebrate it.

So that was great, and he went into the Forthspring and there was a dance for him and all the rest of it – I don't think he actually wanted the dance, but anyway he got what he got – and then going down the Springfield Road together, the Dalai Lama, Barry Dodds and Gerry Reynolds – the three of those going down the road and into another place where there was going to be a celebration at the end of Lanark there, where there was going to be a bit of a service. There was a beautiful picture in the papers of the Dalai Lama in the middle, holding the beards of the two men and a wee twinkle in his eye – he was enjoying it. It was lovely – to me it was a beautiful symbol.

But in the midst of peace violence and disagreement persisted.

Whiterock Parade

There was one very bad one. It was at the 10th anniversary of Forthspring and there was a concert organised for the Saturday night – they had to cancel it because they blocked the roads and the people that were coming to the concert – the choirs and what not - couldn't get in so they had to cancel it. And then the next day – the Sunday was a big celebration. So we had parked our car in the grounds here at the back and we were advised to go up to Cornerstone and stay up in Cornerstone that night – the Saturday night. So we went up to Cornerstone and stayed the night in Cornerstone but there was no trouble. But the next morning I had asked a friend to pick us up at half past eight so that we could get down to church and George picked us up outside Cornerstone and he said, "Lanark way is closed. I'll have to go down the West Circular" So he drove down the West Circular and I could not believe it. I had never seen anything like that – it was just like a battleground because of what had happened and I think it was the anger over the parade. They nearly brought the gates down in Workman Avenue that night. They climbed to the top of the green gates that night and that's why the people told us to go to Cornerstone, to stay in their house. But nothing happened to the house; the house was okay.

That was one of the worst disturbances of the parades. But even that has calmed down a bit. When you would go out and the gate would be open for the short time for the parade to go through, with only the Orangemen allowed through; the parade wasn't allowed through. You would have heard jeering on the other side but later you didn't hear the jeering – it seemed to be a silent protest. So there are things happening and things are changing all the time. I would just love to see those gates opened. That would be a great joy to see, well, we were there when they were closed for so many years and it would be a joy to have them opened... but whether it'll be in our time or not, who knows.

As life became relatively calm people looked back on the period of intense conflict often, it seemed, with a sense of bewilderment.

How Did We Cope?

I don't know. I don't know how anybody coped. I often say that even now, "How did we cope?" and if it ever, God forbid, should happen again, should we ever cope again? I don't think I could because I keep saying if anything like that ever happened again I wouldn't be here; I'd get out. When you're younger you can sort of make your way through it but I think, as you get older, you just don't want that. I don't think anybody wants that for at the time it was bad enough. It's when you've young children, you're afraid for them. It would be my grandchildren who I would worry about. I know the older one is very sensible but it would be the younger grandchildren – the teenagers, it would them. But in saying that, it wouldn't be the troubles now you have to worry about. It's fellows from within the community – among each other. I think now Protestant and Catholic are starting to come together, which is a good thing, I can see a lot of friendships being made through that... but it's coming now from within our own community.

For some people their response to the conflict was to find opportunities to build bridges, to engage with people from different backgrounds and communities.

Forthspring

I used to go to the Curragh first and it had meetings on a Wednesday morning with Sister Noreen and it went from there. Somebody asked me to go, on a Wednesday morning and I thought, "Ach well, sure I'll go." I wasn't working now and I said I'd go round and it just went from there. Noreen was very nice. It snowballed just from that. They would have gone out to places for the day and I'm an outdoor person, I love being outdoors. Then we went to Scotland and we got intouch with Dublin and we would have gone down to Dublin and they would have come up to visit us.

I've never let myself or my family get involved with things like that because they went up to the Springfield School and I've always taught them that everybody's the same. My son, he works downtown and there's a fellow who is Egyptian and he said to me, 'Flippin' foreigners. You see these Egyptians and all' you see, he was very arrogant there for a while and I said, 'Just take him as he is.' So he comes in the other day and says, 'You know, mummy, he brought me a pen back – he was over in Egypt visiting his family and he brought me a pen and a notebook back and he also brought me cigarettes.' I replied to him, 'Didn't I tell you that there was good in everybody; but you couldn't see it because you just had this thing against foreigners taking over jobs.' I've never taught my children to be sectarian or racist or anything like that.

I just hope and pray that things will never go back to the time when people have to lose their children through sectarian violence but saying that, they fight amongst each other anyway as a fellow my grandson knows was on the Shankill and he happened to say something and all these fellows beat him up – he was 28 – and he ended up in hospital there. If they're in clubs on their own side even and they've had too much to drink and they come out with something wrong, they're getting beat up – and that was only about two weeks ago and I think he had to get stitches in his eye and stitches in his head.

Despite some reservations this woman expresses the view that life has improved during the Peace Process.

Since the Good Friday Agreement

Things are a lot better. There is no rioting, there is peace, it is quiet. It's great, children go out now. You don't even think about it, they go out, they come back. Life is much more relaxed. But what I will say since the army is no longer on the streets it's not as safe for girls; there are more crimes against women. There is less likelihood of people getting caught. The physical attacks on women have increased.

You are still getting young people shot, young people brutalized. They are still trying to attack policemen, both sides. So I wouldn't call it a complete peace process. But it is good that mothers can let their teenagers go out and not have to worry because in my day it was different. But I wonder if there will ever be peace. Young people are mixing more now. They go into the town and go to bars and clubs, wherever they go to now, and get on with each other. The town is much busier now.

This young man reflects on how the Troubles influenced his life, the impact of peace and his hopes for the future.

The Troubles shaped my life

The Troubles shaped my life... around our area there was a lot of youth clubs. We would go to the youth clubs a lot so your parents would know that you were safe. I think maybe the young people before me have been hindered by the Troubles. A lot of them wouldn't have wanted to leave the area – I still know people who wouldn't even leave the Springfield Road. So, I think there are people who shut themselves away and maybe don't know what's out there and don't know what is good for them. And if you look, on the other hand, my great-grandfather emigrated to other countries – sometimes for the best, sometimes for the worst – it has happened.

You always hung about in your own area but I think as it went on people got more confident and if you heard if one of your friends was in the town – that was brilliant. It made you confident and it made you want to explore where you are and what else was out there. And then you're meeting the other community, you're meeting different communities and ethnic minorities and you ask yourself, "What was all the fuss about in the first place?"

It was about that stage the Good Friday agreement had come along there was a more peaceful society. You had people from all over the world starting to come when you're 19 or 20 and I just had a good buzz about the whole of Belfast and going into the town and feeling safe and stuff.

I'm 26 now – I'd say between the ages of 21 and 24 it was looking very bright and really good; I thought everything was going in the right direction but now I don't know where it's going to go because there's different things happening and the politicians aren't strong enough. I don't feel they're actually developing the country now.

I'd like to see some of the peace walls getting smaller – I'm not saying taken away because maybe people's safety would be at risk. I'd also like to see more inter-community schools and youth clubs. Hopefully people could live together – that would be another wish. It would be good if people could respect each other more.

This woman considers the changes as the Troubles have came to an end.

We're A Bit Happier

Honestly, I sometimes say to myself, I know I've lived through it and all but I think it has taught us to appreciate more – appreciate life now as it is, you know, our kids are grown up now and they have kids of their own. During the Troubles you didn't have time to appreciate your children as you were always saying to them, "Get you in", "Get you up the stairs", "Don't you be going out", "Where did he go?", "Where did she go?", etc. You were sort of hounding your kids then, whereas now the kids have that wee bit of freedom and if they are out late you're not worried so much. We have a wee grandson who comes to stay, he comes in at 10:30, but if he's five minutes late it used to be, "Oh my God, where is he?" where now you're saying to yourself, he'll be alright – he's held up and you can relax. Back then if he had been five minutes late you would've been ringing the hospitals but that's all gone now. We're a bit happier.

CHAPTER 5
Life during the Troubles

A number of features emerge across the stories. The determination of people to live what they describe as 'ordinary lives'. Lives not shaped or determined by the conflict. The resilience of people is a feature, their determination to keep going in what seem like unbearable circumstances. However this has to be set alongside an increasing sense of emotional and physical wear and tear as the conflict deepened and lengthened over time. By the 1980's there is a marked sense of bleakness, gone is the excitement of the earlier, deadlier days and there is a wide spread dependency on prescription drugs as a means of dealing with the constant stress, strain and pain. People's sense of humour always shines through. As does the diversity and complexity of people's lives. They rarely fit neatly into stereotypes or the political or sectarian jigsaw. There is a spirit of generosity and a capacity to understand the perspectives of others.

The experience of people born outside the North but who choose to live in Northern Ireland during the period of the Troubles is relatively untold. This woman came to the North and, in doing so, found friends and a way to navigate what to others would have seemed impossible religious and political boundaries.

Dublin to Belfast

I thought well at least I'd stay a year in Belfast and I'm still here now at nearly 83 years of age. I find Belfast terribly friendly and I've never had problems. They told me to keep my voice down when I came, they were afraid of my Dublin accent being heard in town. An interesting thing was my relationship with the Unionists, I had hardly ever met one in Dublin, but I was doing courses when I came – one was aromatherapy – and I did some of it in the Windsor Women's Centre here in the Village. I was a bit startled, I hadn't realised that Broadway curls around and goes into the very heart of UFF territory. When I saw this mural on the wall, a twenty foot UFF mural, it was so funny I learned it off by heart. I recited it at a Republican dinner in honour of 1916 in Dublin.

I was a bit shocked where the Windsor Women's Centre is, it seemed to be very dilapidated that street, a lot of houses seem to be empty. I wondered is it safe. My republican friends said what on earth are you doing there with your Dublin accent and everything, it's not safe. So anyway, they were so nice to me and welcomed me. They looked at me as their pet fenian you know and we had great fun. It had been burnt down after Mary McAleese had opened it. I couldn't speak too highly of them, we had great fun. Many of the girls began to tell me their problems, about their dads who were in the RUC or UDA or UFF and had to sleep with revolvers under their pillow every night. And we made a great friendship.

The capacity to keep going comes through strongly in the stories people tell of their lives during the conflict.

Resilience

A participant commented that there is a 'bit of fight in everybody who came through the Troubles'. Another woman comments, however, that there was wear and tear over time, 'by the 80's we were all on Prozac.' Participants frequently asked 'how did we live through that'? There answer was a mixture of their determination and the support of family and the local community. Times of hardship were recalled as times of pulling together. One woman recalled the UWC strike with affection: 'we were all out on the street. We had one fire, everybody cooked on it. A bread van was hi-jacked, it was all shared out'. Another spoke of carrying on working during Bloody Friday, saying you had to keep on functioning some way, though acknowledging it was hard for the people at home waiting for your return from work. There is a sense of the resilience and endurance in one woman's memories of her family who were burnt out from Saunders Street on the Newtownards Road in the 1920's, moved to the Donegal Road and then to Haypark Avenue on the Ormeau Road, to be forced from there in the 1970's, ending up in Ballymurphy. But resilience can collapse in to numbness, one woman spoke of 'death washing over you, you got used to it'.

A feature of many of the stories is the concern for others. Mothers worried for their children, almost constantly it seems.

A Concern for Others

It was a worrying time for everybody because, as I said, my child was taken off the bus and interrogated. When my children went out in the morning with all the shooting at that particular time and with people just being in the wrong place at the wrong time, you were worried until your children came home and if they went out at night you did not sleep. And that was everybody – you did not sleep until your child came in.

That was the worst time – the teenagers. Because you would have heard on the TV that night that somebody was shot. There were two fellows stick out in my mind– I didn't know them – but I'm sure you remember them, they were 19 and 20 and they were students – they were Catholics and those two fellows were just walking through. They weren't doing anybody any harm. And it must have been devastating. I felt for the parents because when you have children of your own and they're out you knew what it was like.

I remember William was late one night coming in and Billy went over to the police station because we had no phone at that time. He went over and got them to go out and look for him. About ten minutes later he walked in – I could have killed him. But it was worrying – it was a worrying time. Thankfully none of mine were hurt or injured in these Troubles; it must have been awful for the people whose sons and daughters were in the wrong place at the wrong time.

This woman describes a neighbour who, despite personal risk, felt compelled to reach out to another human being.

Peace to live

The soldiers became targets too. I met one woman – a soldier was shot and was dying – and she went out and put a pillow under his head and a blanket round him and she held him till the ambulance came and that woman never got peace to live, but never gave in. You know, she held her own and she lived in her house – she's still in it. She ignored them when they shouted at her. One day I heard her turn around and say, "Well, at least I'm a Christian and not like you; I'm not an animal." No matter what your feelings, how could you walk past somebody who was hurt? You couldn't do it. She was in the shop one day and she said, "It could have been my son. That's the way I look at it; it could have been my son."

Generosity could appear from unexpected quarters, often provided at considerable personal risk. In this particular instance the generosity was seen as having almost mystical or religious origins.

Guardian Angel

My wee boy had a very bad eye. There was a bus which took people down to the Royal Hospital to give blood and I went round. It was like a first aid bus, and I took the wee boy round – he was only about five – and they said, 'look, we're taking people in a bus down to the Royal – we'll take him – you come with him'. I came with him to the Royal and the doctor told me to to stay with him and we'll get the hospital doctor to see him– he was a coloured doctor – he was in doing an operation. He came out and he said, "Oh my god, what an eye" I don't know what it was but it was like he'd been punched in the eye. So he gave him a cream but we waited that long on the doctor coming out of the theatre, when we got out the bus had gone. So I was standing on the Falls Road with the child and it was like a ghost town – I mean there was not one single person on that road. So, these two fellows came in a car – they were workmen – and they said, 'where are you going?' and I said, 'I'm going to Turf Lodge' and they said, 'Get in, we'll bring you up. We're going up that way.' So they were going to Norfolk Glen so they dropped me off and I walked on. But about a few weeks later I brought him back to the hospital as he was to go back again. It was a very strange thing because when I brought him back, they couldn't find the doctor. I had to give a description of the doctor – there was no such doctor on that day, there was no such a doctor in theatre that day of that description and I stood and argued with her and I said, 'well, then, who treated him? Who gave him the ointment for his eye? He definitely did get this ointment and it was a coloured doctor, a young doctor with curly hair.' They didn't know anything but his eye healed up after about three days. I said, 'Oh my god, was that a guardian angel?'

The two workmen who drove us up the road... One was an elderly man and the other was a young fellow. They must have been working but where they were working I don't know because it was really eerie that day. It was about five o' clock. The road – there wasn't a bus, there wasn't a car, there wasn't a taxi – nothing. And I saw the car – and I was ready, prepared to walk when they stopped and said, "Where are you going, we'll take you." which was very good of them.

Statistically men were at much greater risk during the conflict. But the bare statistics do not tell the story of the stress and worry, the pain and the loss, that were endured by men and women both. However, in general, the experience of men and women tended to be different.

Women and the Troubles

You felt safer for women going out – especially young women than young men very much. During the Troubles, I know there were a lot of women killed at the beginning of the Troubles and injured, but at the very start of the

Troubles, there seemed to be a bit more respect for women from everybody, from the Army and whoever else you want to include, but I think that eroded with time. It just seemed like a different world, you know, your freedom all went. You'd have thought nothing of just going for a walk at 8, 9 or 10 o'clock. Everybody went out for a walk and then all of a sudden, no, and you only walked within a certain boundary and you didn't cross boundaries and then I think it just escalated to the point where people in the communities didn't have any contact again.

When I was a teenager, I had a freedom to wander where I wanted, I mean, obviously I had to say where I was going but there was nobody who said, "You can't go here, you can't go there." Whereas with my son, who was born in '73 - I think I drove him to most of the places he was going to, if he was going across town, until he drove himself.

Although segregation increasingly became the norm, with in excess of 90% of the population in working class areas being either predominantly Protestant or Catholic, many people refused to live their lives solely within one community.

Segregation

Protestants were asked if they wanted the houses being built on the Springfield Road but nobody would live there and you could see why. A lot of people moved out, the Protestants moved out and Catholics moved in.

I'm just one of those people – it never annoyed me. I would have walked down and into Lanark way and walked down that way. Well it wasn't Lanark Way but it was Merkland Street or something like that, but I would have walked down that way. When the children were at school, I would have left them up the Springfield Road and walked straight down – nobody ever said anything and I never felt intimidated.

I remember one morning I was coming down and this man was in the car and he was going down and he said to me, 'Do you know where the Royal is?' to which I replied, 'Aye, I'll hop in' to show him and he said, 'You could have been anybody.' He left me to the Blackstaff.

A lot of people wouldn't even go into town when the troubles started because they were really afraid. Everybody's different. They wouldn't have gone into town in case a bomb went off. I just took the attitude: you get on with it.

In the midst of extraordinarily difficult times people retained a sense of humour and often recalled the events of the Troubles with some of that humour.

Humour

One participant recalled getting into an argument with a local character known as 'Two guns', not, the storyteller remarked, a very encouraging nickname. A woman had a colleague in her office who cried out, 'Oh, Mummy', each time a bomb went off, a not infrequent occurrence, prompting another worker to ask her eventually if it was her Mummy who was planting all the bombs. Another recalled with a smile the arrest of a neighbour due to the quantity of sugar found under her bed. She was a baker and was hoarding the sugar. Not, as suspected, a bomb maker. Following a bomb on the Shankill that had destroyed a jewellery shop a woman recalled meeting a friend dressed, she said, 'like Mr. T'. A young man was stopped by the soldiers in the middle of summer and asked what he had in his lunch box, 'Snowballs'[11] was the reply. They thought he was being funny and gave him a kicking.

There was a widespread cynicism about the effectiveness of security measures. It was common knowledge that you could avoid the queues at the High Street security barriers by nipping through Woolworths. Politicians today might be comforted by the fact that their peers before and during the Troubles were not held in particularly high esteem. The Unionist Party was described as a 'corrupt lot'. One man recalled a rhyme he learnt from his father: 'I have come before you, To stand behind you, To tell you something, I know nothing about'. One woman, no fan of Ian Paisley, commented that he was 'rank poison...his voice would have cracked coalbrick'. Though there were honourable mentions for working class politicians such as Paddy Devlin and John McQuade.

There was an unsurprising obsession with news during the Troubles. In the absence of a 24 hour news culture people relied on the 'jungle telegraph', local word of mouth communication. Many people listened to police short band radio. Staying up to hear the final news bulletin on the television was a matter of routine for people in the days when television channels closed down, often before midnight with the playing of the British national anthem.

11 A popular bun, covered in coconut.

Communication and News

One woman recalled the compulsion to hear the news before bed but observed 'I always hated turning the news on – it was always terrible'. Another said you had to know what happened. She remembers as a child, sitting on the outside toilet with her mother listening to the police radio.

This woman's obsession with the police radio led her on to Citizen Band.

Citizen Band Radio

My great aunt lived in Cupar Street. When I went over they would have minded me when my parents were at work. They had a big radio with a handle on it, like a big box with thick knobs. My great uncle would have sat each night listening to it. You would have heard the police messages 'Going up the Shankill Road, such and such....there is a standoff there'. If you heard someone's name mentioned you would have run to their house to warn them. I used to love sitting listening to it. Then the CB's started to come out, Citizen Band. My sister-in-law was on them and I got a lend of one and I was hooked. It was like Facebook. Whatever you were saying other people listened in. I was talking to people from Taughmonagh, Donegall Road, all across the city and then I met my husband through it. I went to a party and I met him in person. He already knew me. I was Hotlips. That was my handle.

The most frequent observation on the Troubles was 'never again'. Participants, however they described what had happened or why it had happened, overwhelmingly shared the view that they did not want their children or grandchildren to have to live through anything similar again.

Reflections on the Troubles

The Troubles as a period was always recalled with regret and a sense of horror. A common sentiment was 'Thank God it's all over'. One man's initial thoughts were that it would be all over in a month or two. Another, looking back, observed that the 'Troubles kicked off and changed everything'. They were in the words of various participants 'hell', 'damnable days'. There was collective relief that is was all over, 'it was no easy time'.

There was what might be described as an ambiguous relationship to the rule of law as lines became blurred with the onset of violence and chaos.

Lawlessness

One woman recalled what she said was the common practice of people going in to a shop as a friend phoned in a bomb scare and you walked out with a new suit. Looting was common, either during riots or following bombing of commercial property. 'We had orange juice for a month' was one memory, another was of an oversupply of pineapples following an explosion at a greengrocers. A young woman recalled her granny with her apron full of stones to provide ammunition to men who were rioting.

A recurring theme was the role of fate, being either in the wrong place at the wrong time or narrowly missing death or injury.

Fate

Participants often focused on either good or bad fortune. Being 'in the wrong place at the wrong time' or haunted by how accidental events were, how, 'but for the grace of God' they might have ended up dead or severely injured. Time and time again in the telling of stories and in the remembering the role of fate was referred to. At one level it seemed to be recognition of the randomness of it all, a way of acknowledging and coping with the chaos people lived through and at another level a despairing attempt to explain the inexplicable. How could people enact such violence on each other?

In the telling of stories participants displayed a generosity and level of understanding of the perspective of others that would run counter to the view that communities in interface areas live in parallel universes.

Generosity and Understanding

One woman spoke of listening to her Catholic work mates describing raids by the army and expressed her lack of surprise that they ended up supporting the IRA. Another talked of grievances in the 60's, 'Catholics thought we were gifted, we got the best of everything. That wasn't true but there were grounds for trouble'. She said that the civil rights marchers were attacked and that was wrong. Many participants expressed an awareness of the level of fear felt not only in their own community but in the other community: Catholic fear of loyalist paramilitaries and the security forces, Protestant fear of the IRA.

Conclusion

In the Chorus from "The Cure of Troy" Seamus Heaney says how

> Human beings suffer,
> They torture one another,
> They get hurt and get hard....

Yet it is a tribute to so many people who participated in this project that they have avoided getting hard. They have looked out for themselves and their families as best they can and reached out to others, in many cases across the communal divide.

The chorus continues:

> So hope for a great sea change
> On the far side of revenge

Although there has not yet been a great sea change in relationships along the peace wall dividing the Shankill and Falls, thanks to the generosity of many, there has been a calming of the waters, the beginnings of a new set of relationships. For many people they are content to live within the existing divisions but for those who wish to move beyond them there is a recognition that we need to hear and understand each other's accounts of the past.

Bibliography

An Crann Bear in Mind 2000

An Crann Crossings 2001

Ardoyne Commemoration Project Ardoyne: The Untold Truth 2002

Barnes, J The Sense of an Ending 2011

Bishop,P., Mallie, E, The Provisional IRA 1988

Kerr, M The Destructors 2011

McKittrick, D, Kelters, S, Feeny, B, Thornton, C and McVea D Lost Lives 2008

McKittrick, D McVea, D Making Sense of the Troubles 2001

O'Doherty M The Telling Year: Belfast 1972 2007

Rolston, B Children of the Revolution 2011

Smyth, M Fay, M-T Personal Accounts from Northern Ireland's Troubles 2000

Taylor, P. Provos The IRA and Sinn Fein 1998

Wharton, K Sir, They're Taking the Kids Indoors: The British Army in Northern Ireland, 1973/74 2012